The Academic Administrator and the Law
What Every Dean and Department Chair Needs to Know

J. Douglas Toma and Richard L. Palm

ASHE-ERIC Higher Education Report Volume 26, Number 5

Prepared by

ERIC Clearinghouse on Higher Education
URL: www.eriche.org

In cooperation with

*Association for the Study
of Higher Education*
URL: http://www.tiger.coe.missouri.edu/~ashe

Published by

*Graduate School of Education and Human Development
The George Washington University*
URL: www.gwu.edu

Adrianna J. Kezar, Series Editor

Cite as

Toma, J. Douglas, and Richard L. Palm. 1999. *The Academic Administrator and the Law: What Every Dean and Department Chair Needs to Know.* ASHE-ERIC Higher Education Report Volume 26, No. 5. Washington, D.C.: The George Washington University, Graduate School of Education and Human Development.

Library of Congress Catalog Card Number 98-88006
ISSN 0884-0040
ISBN 1-878380-85-0

Managing Editor: Lynne J. Scott
Manuscript Editor: Barbara M. Fishel
Cover Design by Michael David Brown, Inc., The Red Door Gallery, Rockport, ME

The ERIC Clearinghouse on Higher Education invites individuals to submit proposals for writing monographs for the *ASHE-ERIC Higher Education Report* series. Proposals must include:
1. A detailed manuscript proposal of not more than five pages.
2. A chapter-by-chapter outline.
3. A 75-word summary to be used by several review committees for the initial screening and rating of each proposal.
4. A vita and a writing sample.

ERIC Clearinghouse on Higher Education
Graduate School of Education and Human Development
The George Washington University
One Dupont Circle, Suite 630
Washington, DC 20036-1183

This publication was prepared partially with funding from the Office of Educational Research and Improvement, U.S. Department of Education, under contract no. ED RR-93-002008. The opinions expressed in this report do not necessarily reflect the positions or policies of OERI or the Department.

EXECUTIVE SUMMARY

The deans and chairs who direct academic programs at universities, colleges, and community colleges frequently must address issues that raise legal questions. It is difficult to name a program or a service in higher education that does not intersect with the law in some way. The academic administrator must develop the skills needed to recognize the legal issues that invariably shape the policies and decisions made in a school or department. And deans and chairs must understand the resources available to assist them in resolving these issues, particularly when to call for legal advice.

What Legal Issues Might Arise for Deans and Chairs?

A variety of legal issues are likely to arise in university and college schools and departments. The most common ones involve contract and tort matters for staff and students, constitutional or statutory due process and equal protection, free expression, and external regulation in areas such as immigration and copyrights. The sources of the law that govern these issues are also numerous, ranging from the U.S. Constitution and the constitutions of the states, to state and federal legislation and administrative rule making, to judicial decisions made at all levels, to institutional rules and regulations, to institutional custom and practice.

Does the Legal Community Defer to Academic Decision Making?

Common across all types of legal issues, sources of law, and institutions is a traditional legislative and judicial deference to academic decision making. Though this traditional deference has eroded over time, it remains pronounced across higher education. But despite the considerable autonomy the law has customarily afforded higher education, it treats public and private institutions differently, and it applies different rules to religious and secular universities and colleges. In particular, public institutions are subject to constitutional provisions.

What Are the Roles of Institutional Counsel and Academic Deans and Chairs?

Academic administrators must not only know what the law is, but also understand the roles of counsel and the procedural contexts within which lawyers work. Deans and chairs frequently work with attorneys, both those retained by the institution and those hired in a personal capacity. These lawyers perform a variety of functions, and they owe their loyalty to different institutional clients at different times. One factor is relatively constant, however: Information exchanged between counsel and client is privileged and cannot be divulged.

Also of interest to academic administrators are the actual process of litigation—from complaint and answer, to discovery and trial (or settlement), to decision and remedy—and the issues of authority and delegation that determine whether individuals or institutions will be held liable.

What Issues Do Academic Administrators Face Daily?
The essence of the relationship between employers and employees is the employment contract, whether within the context of one-on-one bargaining between two parties or as part of a broader collective bargaining agreement. Closely related to employment contracts are decisions about hiring and promotion, each of which raises issues of equal protection and due process, particularly given constitutional provisions and statutory protections under the antidiscrimination laws. Moreover, these same issues commonly arise in matters of reappointment, tenure, promotion, and the dismissal and retirement of tenured faculty and staff. Affirmative action frequently plays a role in the employment relationship.

Academic administrators must keep in mind several very practical concerns in hiring and promoting faculty and staff: avoiding inappropriate questions during the interview, respecting individual privacy rights, and following immigration laws. Deans and chairs must also understand and respect faculty members' right of academic freedom while still evaluating faculty performance, taking action when it is insufficient, and investigating and perhaps punishing misconduct by employees, such as sexual harassment.

Courts increasingly decide cases involving students using implied contract theories, having moved from the traditional doctrine of in loco parentis. Institutions are no longer necessarily assumed to have a parental-type relationship with students. Students are viewed as consumers with reasonable expectations of institutions for programs and services. In addition, although the traditional deference to academic decision making persists, courts are ever more willing to intervene in campus disciplinary actions involving both academic concerns and disciplinary matters. Typically, the key question in disciplinary matters is due process: How much notice and how much process is a student entitled to in a given situation?

Similarly, although courts continue to afford broad discretion to academic administrators in the area of admissions, institutions may be held in violation of the antidiscrimination laws and Equal Protection Clause of the U.S. Constitution when they act in a discriminatory manner, including in the emerging area of disability. Immigration law is also a common issue in admissions. Deans and chairs must also be aware of legislation that governs the confidentiality of students' records, as well as constitutional provisions that protect the right of students to organize and express themselves. Finally, negligence-based institutional liability involving students is a critical concern for academic administrators.

Several state and federal regulations have a substantial effect on administrative decisions for schools and departments, particularly those addressing intellectual property, open meetings, family and medical leave, funded research, and taxation. Similarly, schools and departments are typically heavily involved in accreditation coordinated by private associations that serve a quasi-regulatory function.

The Academic Administrator and the Law includes an extensive list of references that provide more detailed analysis of particular topics. In no way is the report intended to be a substitute for sound legal advice, nor can it answer all legal questions a dean or chair might have. It does provide the background needed to better understand the complex relationships between the law and the administration of academic services and programs in postsecondary education.

CONTENTS

Foreword	**ix**
Acknowledgments	**xi**
Introduction	**1**
The Law, the Courts, and Counsel	**5**
Types of Legal Issues	5
Internal and External Sources of the Law	8
Deference to Academic and Behavioral Decisions	9
The Distinction between Public and Private Institutions	12
The Attorney-Client Relationship	14
Pretrial and Trial Procedures	17
Individual or Institutional Liability: Authority and Delegation	22
The Employment Relationship with Faculty and Staff	**27**
Foundations of the Relationship between Employer and Employee	27
Hiring and Promotion Decisions: Equal Protection and Due Process	30
Practical Concerns in Hiring and Promotion	51
Conduct and Misconduct on the Job: Navigating the Employment Relationship	60
Dismissal and Retirement of Faculty and Staff	74
Students in the Academic Setting	**85**
Contract, Consumerism, and Citizenship	85
Misconduct and Discipline	89
Admissions and Access	93
Students' Records	101
Expression, Organizations, and Publications	103
Institutional Liability	108
Regulation and Oversight in the School and the Department	**111**
Copyrights, Trademarks, and Patent Law	111
Openness and Disclosure	114
Family and Medical Leave	115
Research and Teaching	116
Taxation and Fundraising	119
Accreditation	121
References	**125**
Index	**151**

ASHE-ERIC Higher Education Reports   **167**
Advisory Board   169
Consulting Editors   171
Review Panel   175
Recent Titles   177
Order Form

FOREWORD

In many ways, higher education institutions have remained protected from the onslaught of lawsuits prevalent in so many sectors of our society. Nevertheless, college and university administrators need to become concerned about the steady erosion of the traditional protections against lawsuits that institutions have relied on.

Structural changes, such as the breakdown of traditional selection and acculturation processes, greater recognition of constitutional and contractual rights, the decline of career mobility for faculty, a greater array of service functions for higher education institutions, the increase in both external and internal regulation, and the technology revolution, have contributed to colleges' and universities' increased involvement in litigation. Accordingly, many campuses are refining their campus affirmative action, sexual harassment, disciplinary, technology, due process, discrimination, and athletics policies as new cases reshape our understanding of these areas of law.

Higher education professionals need to understand the impact of this growing litigious environment on their roles. They need to learn how to handle a growing number of legal dilemmas. Institutions need to consider whether their rules and policies adequately minimize their legal exposure in areas such as scope of employment, nongovernmental functions, foundations and related activities, cost of defense, out-of-state activities, and liability insurance. Deans and department chairs are the ones most often on the front line, with responsibility for legal issues surrounding employment relationships, students, and research, and for school and departmental issues such as accreditation and copyrights. Deans' and department chairs' administrative activities must be examined and considered daily in the context of legal issues that might be related. A handbook from human resources personnel or even from legal counsel will not adequately prepare an academic administrator for this job.

Thankfully, *The Academic Administrator and the Law,* by J. Douglas Toma and Richard L. Palm, assists by providing the context needed to address these important concerns. Moreover, it fills the information gap between a handbook from legal counsel and legal textbooks, providing a more generalized, nonlegalese discussion and offering a broad understanding of the complex legal situation facing higher education institutions.

Toma and Palm, both assistant professors of higher education at the University of Missouri–Kansas City, have synthesized the key literature relevant to legal issues that academic administrators encounter daily. They introduce basic legal principles and interpret the judicial process. One of the most important lessons embedded in *The Academic Administrator and the Law* is that deans and chairs must become aware of the legal implications of an issue. Moreover, once they discover an issue, they must know how to work effectively with legal counsel. The authors' goal of having academic administrators become active participants in resolving legal issues and implementing preventive legal strategies is particularly important in an environment of growing litigiousness.

The Academic Administrator and the Law examines legal issues and how they vary by institutional type and institutional context. It offers specific information for church-affiliated institutions, public institutions, and private institutions. It also sheds light on timely issues such as affirmative action, the Americans with Disabilities Act, post-tenure review, and immigration, all of which are discussed elsewhere from a mostly philosophical perspective but also have important legal and practical implications.

The scrutiny of employment issues is critical at this time, when faculty members' mobility has declined and litigation is increasing steadily. Toma and Palm's report is a helpful supplement to a previous monograph in the ASHE-ERIC Report series, *Tenure, Promotion, and Reappointment* (vol. 24, no. 1), which details the history of tenure, the development of faculty employment contracts, constitutional rights in employment, discrimination in employment, and peer review.

Legal issues will only become more prevalent and more complex. Toma and Palm's report will help administrators, especially academic leaders, to become more aware of the ways that a legal perspective can enhance their effectiveness and their accountability as agents of the institution. Astute academic leaders will value the synthesis and analysis of important legal issues contained in *The Academic Administrator and the Law*.

Adrianna J. Kezar
Series Editor,
Assistant Professor of Higher Education, and
Director, ERIC Clearinghouse on Higher Education

ACKNOWLEDGMENTS

Our deep thanks go to several people who made our work possible and enjoyable.

Alan Douglas went well above and beyond the call of duty as our research assistant on the project.

Linda Edwards, as interim dean at the School of Education, University of Missouri–Kansas City, made available the funds needed to collect binders full of photocopied articles and a shelf full of books and monographs. She has been an invaluable supporter of both this project and our careers in general. Thanks are also due to Bernie Oliver and Ed Underwood, our school dean and department chair, for their advocacy and backing.

The staff in the business office at the School of Education, Brenda Fasken, Brenda Fox, and Paula Specil, did the nearly impossible and sorted though our various receipts and purchase orders.

Adrianna Kezar and the staff at the ERIC Clearinghouse on Higher Education were especially generous in their encouragement of the project and indispensable in readying it for printing. Several reviewers also improved the project greatly through their thoughtful comments on both the proposal and the manuscript.

Finally, the contributions of Carol Palm and Linda Bachman cannot be overestimated. Both offered support in countless important ways throughout the project.

INTRODUCTION

A multitude of legal issues commonly involve chairs of departments and divisions, and deans of colleges and schools at American universities, colleges, and community colleges. We have three main purposes for exploring these issues through what scholars have written about them.

First is to provide academic administrators with the general background necessary to recognize legal issues when they emerge on campus and to develop an appreciation of the resources—whether the books, chapters, articles, and papers synthesized in this report or the legal counsel employed or retained by all institutions—available to assist them in attempts to resolve the problems.

Second is to encourage academic administrators to be active participants in resolving legal issues that arise at a school or in a department. Being somewhat familiar with the essentials of the law—the terminology, procedures, and doctrines—affords the academic administrator the background necessary to be an active consumer of legal advice, whether disseminated through writings or imparted by counsel. Our goal is to afford practicing administrators not only the background to recognize legal issues when they emerge on campus, but also the competence and confidence to engage in sophisticated discussions about them with counsel and colleagues.

Third is to prompt academic administrators to consider and implement preventive law strategies. Potential legal ramifications should be a factor to consider in making decisions within academic units. In other words, the best way to address legal concerns is to anticipate, and thus possibly avoid, legal action. The successful dean or chair should understand the law sufficiently to craft policies that will avoid litigation to the extent possible. But academic administrators should also know enough to recognize that being called into court is quite often a part of their job and that the potential for legal action should not become something that causes paralysis in taking necessary action.

The focus of this report is on legal issues affecting schools or departments at higher education institutions. Although we discuss student issues, a broader literature is available on legal issues in student affairs administration outside the context of the academic unit. For instance, issues involving search and seizure in residence halls are typically outside the responsibility of chairs and deans. The topics that are covered in this report involving students—admissions, student programs, First

Amendment issues—regularly, or at least sometimes, cross the desks of deans and chairs.

Similarly, we cover personnel issues involving faculty and other employees and address external regulation and oversight, but we do not highlight topics—or the technical aspects of topics—that are not typically within the scope of deans' and chairs' duties. Deans and chairs need to be aware of these topics—hiring, academic freedom, promotion and tenure, discipline and dismissal, open meetings and records acts, copyrights, cost recovery, selling and purchasing—but need not always be expert in the intricacies of these matters. Instead, academic administrators need to know which administrators on campus—in student affairs or human resources, for example—have appropriate expertise and when to turn to them with questions. They need to know when to consult the institution's legal counsel, retained to develop a deep understanding of the legal issues that frequently occur in higher education. Still, deans and chairs may often have to interpret and approve procedures that can deeply affect practices in areas like hiring, promotion, and tenure that often involve legal issues. Thus, the intention here is to provide the background that deans and chairs require to recognize potential legal problems—before they arise and as they arise—and the ability needed to ask the appropriate experts on campus the right questions in an attempt to resolve them.

Academic administrators are fortunate that they have several excellent sources of information available on higher education law. The most comprehensive text on the topic is *The Law of Higher Education* (Kaplin and Lee 1995), which explores the entire range of issues in higher education law. Another important resource is *The Law and Higher Education* (Olivas 1997), which contains edited court decisions illustrating the issues occurring within higher education interspersed with commentary. Robert Hendrickson annually reviews developments in higher education law in *Yearbook of Education Law* (Russo 1996). Finally, several newsletters available by subscription provide monthly, bimonthly, or quarterly updates on current developments in higher education law, explaining current cases decided in the courts and their potential application and impact on campus.

A fine scholarly journal, *Journal of College and University Law,* carries articles on current issues in higher education law and publishes an annual review of changes. Articles in the *Journal,* typically found in law libraries and the offices of institutional counsel, generally walk a line between theory and practical advice. Similarly, law reviews—journals edited by law students that include theory-focused articles by both law students and legal scholars—and education journals collected in the ERIC database routinely publish articles related to legal issues at universities, colleges, and community colleges. Articles on law in education journals are generally more user-friendly and for nonlawyers than articles in law reviews.

Finally, several national organizations—the National Association of College and University Attorneys (NACUA), the College and University Personnel Association (CUPA), the National Association of Student Personnel Administrators (NASPA), the American College Personnel Association (ACPA), for example—disseminate updates on legal issues of note to academic administrators. These organizations also periodically produce monographs or edited collections covering specific issues in higher education law. Such publications generally take a practical approach to legal issues and are usually written for the nonlawyer. Each of these associations has an Internet site that includes a list of its publications.

THE LAW, THE COURTS, AND COUNSEL

The academic administrator is likely to have a variety of types of legal issues cross his or her desk, which may be grounded in contract or tort, constitution or statute, or any number of other bases. The sources of the laws that govern these issues are also numerous, ranging from the U.S. Constitution and the state constitutions, to state and federal legislation and administrative rule making, to judicial decisions made at all levels, to institutional rules and regulations, to institutional custom and practice. Common across these types of legal issues and sources of law, and across different types of institutions, is a traditional legislative and judicial deference to academic decision making. Though this traditional deference has eroded over time, it remains pronounced across higher education. Although the law has customarily afforded higher education considerable autonomy, it treats public and private institutions differently, and it applies different rules to religious and secular universities and colleges; that is, public institutions are subject to constitutional provisions.

Academic administrators must not only know what the law is, but also understand the roles of counsel and the procedural contexts within which lawyers work. Deans and chairs frequently work with attorneys, both those retained by the institution and those hired by the academic administrator in a personal capacity. These lawyers perform a variety of functions, and campus counsel owe their loyalty to different clients within the institution at different times. One fact is relatively constant, however: Information exchanged in the course of the relationship between counsel and client is privileged. Also of interest to academic administrators are the actual process of litigation—from complaint and answer, through discovery and trial (or settlement), to decision and remedies—and the issues of authority and delegation that determine whether individuals or institutions will be held liable.

Types of Legal Issues

Several types of legal issues commonly require the attention of academic administrators—contractual issues (often involving personnel matters, but also connected with complaints by students), tort issues, constitutional concerns such as equal protection, due process, or free expression, and administrative rules and regulations.

Contractual issues are among the most common legal issues that deans and chairs confront. A contract involves a set of promises that create a duty of performance under the law and the right to a legal remedy when they are breached. Personnel issues often revolve around interpretations of an employment contract. Matters involving employment are often heated and are sometimes concerns of great magnitude, as in disputes between faculty and institutions over the denial of tenure or outright dismissal. Employee grievance and arbitration procedures, as well as issues involving employee benefits, are also contractual in nature. Such issues are incorporated into individual contracts—either as direct provisions or by reference as general institutional rules and regulations—or are included in collective bargaining agreements that structure the employment relationship for entire groups of employees. And many actions brought by students, particularly at private schools, are based in contract provisions. These actions rely on the premise that catalogs and other materials produced by an institution contain promises that the institution must keep.

Issues involving torts sometimes arise for deans and chairs. A tort involves damage to someone resulting from the nonperformance of a duty by someone else. Torts involve duties that are not contractual in nature. They result from the reasonable expectation by someone that something done by the defendant—either some act or some failure to act—will not be the proximate cause of some damage incurred by him or her. Defamation—an intentional false communication, written (libel) or spoken (slander), made by someone to a third party that injures the reputation or good name of another—is one example of misconduct by an employee of the school or department that would be classified as a tort.

Several constitutional-type issues can originate among units in higher education. The guarantees under the Fourteenth Amendment to the U.S. Constitution of equal protection and due process are often the basis for a plaintiff's allegations of discrimination against public institutions. The theory underlying equal protection is that the government should not treat similarly situated individuals differently, unless it has a very good reason to do so, such as affirmative action. Due process is protection against the government's depriving any individual of life, liberty, or property without adequate notice and an adequate hearing. Constitutional provisions protect against actions by the state, including officials of public universities, colleges, and community colleges, against the rights of individuals but do not extend to private institutions. In other words, only the state—or a private entity acting in the place of the state—is subject to the provisions of the Constitution.

Several federal statutes aimed at eliminating discrimination in areas like employment or admissions—Titles VII and IX, the Americans with Disabilities Act (ADA), the Age Discrimination in Employment Act (ADEA)—are founded on logic similar to Fourteenth Amendment principles and generally apply to both public and private institutions. These statutes also frequently govern affirmative action initiatives common across institutions or provide individuals with recourse in the event of alleged sexual harassment.

Another set of constitutional-type issues that arise among institutional units revolves around the First Amendment principles of protection against undue government interference in expression, assembly, and the exercise and establishment of religion. Academic freedom—the principle that higher education faculty should be free to pursue new, controversial ideas in their teaching and research (see Olivas 1993)—is not directly a First Amendment issue but has some basis in First Amendment ideals. Private and public schools alike often incorporate principles of equal protection, due process, and free expression into institutional rules and regulations. The rules thus become binding as contract. Accordingly, academic freedom is one of several doctrines that have both constitutional and contractual foundations. The same is true of due process protection extended to individual students as part of disciplinary actions for academic or behavioral misconduct, and the rights of expression and assembly afforded to student organizations in institutional rules and regulations.

Issues involving the concepts of vagueness and overbreadth sometime occur on campus. These concepts reflect the constitutional principle that rules and regulations crafted by the state must be capable of being readily understood by people (vagueness) and not be so broad as to include an overabundance of possible situations to which they apply (overbreadth).

Finally, administrative rules and regulations that originate with federal, state, and local governments often intersect with the administration of academic units. Immigration law is often relevant to the employment of international faculty, staff, and students. Other administrative-type issues—copyrights, open records, animal rights, taxation, for example—also arise in schools and departments.

Internal and External Sources of the Law
The law does not have a single source but instead is derived from several. The first source is federal and state constitutions, foundations of our most basic rights. The First Amendment freedoms in the U.S. Constitution—speech, assembly, press, religion—and the due process and equal protection guaranteed by the Fourteenth Amendment are the constitutional provisions that most often intersect with unit and institutional administration at colleges and universities. Other constitutional provisions, such as the Fourth Amendment (no unlawful search and seizure) and the Fifth Amendment (cannot compel testimony against oneself), are often relevant in student affairs administration, particularly in residence life, but less often are a matter for deans and chairs. These constitutional rights are the paramount legal authority; all provisions from other sources that conflict with the U.S. Constitution are invalid. The job of the U.S. Supreme Court is to make such determinations. Finally, the constitutions of each of the 50 states contain provisions parallel to the U.S. Constitution, which sometimes provide individuals with even stronger protection than the U.S. Constitution.

The law is also a product of federal and state legislation. Federal statutes include antidiscrimination legislation, the Copyright Act, and the Internal Revenue Code. State statutes include workers compensation laws, commercial codes, and legislation creating public universities. Moreover, legislation creates administrative agencies that determine what the law is. Federal agencies like the Equal Employment Opportunity Commission (EEOC) and the National Labor Relations Board (NLRB) make rules and regulations under which institutions and their administrators must operate. The determinations of these agencies are binding as statutes and reviewable in courts. In addition to rule making, these agencies also engage in adjudication. State public service commissions or state civil service commissions serve a similar function. Although institutions must also abide by certain local ordinances—zoning, for instance—and foreign and international law, they rarely are concerns of deans and chairs (C. Greenleaf 1985).

Over time, a body of judicial interpretations—the state and federal common law—has evolved as another source of the law. The common law is based on the concept of precedent, which guides courts in deciding cases before them by reference to previous decisions on similar issues. Thus, individuals can better predict what courts will do. Much of the law in certain areas—contracts, torts, agencies—is the product of these judicial decisions. Courts also interpret constitutions, legislative statutes, administrative regulations, and municipal ordinances. Although prior judicial decisions from other jurisdictions can be instructive to courts, precedents have a binding effect only in the jurisdiction where the case was heard.

The rules and regulations under which deans and chairs must operate are also derived by institutions themselves. These institutional rules and regulations might be the product of governing boards, or they might be administrative decisions. Adjudicatory bodies, such as grievance committees or student judiciaries, also make decisions that create a type of law specific to the institution. The same is true of contracts—written or implied binding legal arrangements between two or more parties—entered into by institutions.

Finally, established, but not necessarily written, practices and understandings within a particular institution—academic custom and usage—constitute a sort of campus common law that defines what members of the academic community expect of each other and the institution itself. Academic custom and usage is important as a supplement to contractual and other "official" understandings (Kaplin and Lee 1995).

The judiciary's traditional stance has been that higher education is a unique enterprise that should regulate itself, based on tradition and consensus.

Deference to Academic and Behavioral Decisions

The judiciary's traditional stance has been that higher education is a unique enterprise that should regulate itself, based on tradition and consensus. Over the years, courts customarily have deferred to the academic judgment of institutions, avoiding extensive regulation and allowing few official channels through which potential plaintiffs could challenge institutional authority (Kaplin and Lee 1995; Sacken 1992). In *Sweezy v. New Hampshire* (1957), the U.S. Supreme Court echoed this tradition, stating that institutions should have the autonomy to determine who should teach, what they may teach, how they should teach it, and who should be admitted to study it (Araujo 1996; V. Brown 1990). Courts have long embraced the philosophy that, given the unique nature of the academic milieu, educators were better situated than judges and juries to make academic decisions (Leas 1991). Courts traditionally, however, have been less willing to defer to institutions on purely behavioral issues, an area where they view themselves as having ample expertise. Still, disciplinary cases in academe involving some sort of misbehavior are rarely disconnected from academic concerns—plagiarism by students is both a behavioral problem and an academic problem, for instance—so judicial deference has remained widespread.

Judicial deference based on academic expertise and institutional uniqueness traditionally has been complemented by the doctrine of governmental immunity. Under this principle, individuals could not bring certain types of actions against the state unless the state had already waived its immunity. Private institutions traditionally enjoyed a parallel protection under the doctrine of charitable immunity. Although most states have heavily restricted or abrogated charitable immunity in recent years, the concept relieved charitable institutions of tort liability while it was recognized. Similarly, the doctrine of governmental immunity has been weakened in recent years with the inclusion of more types of actions as exceptions to the traditional doctrine.

Similarly, the traditional judicial deference to academic decisions has eroded in recent years as the result of a combination of structural changes in American higher education and the emergence of new forums for raising legal challenges and new legal requirements on institutions. Some of these new forums and new requirements are the result of the federal government's greater direct involvement in higher education. One prominent area of increased government involvement in the conduct of a university has been though the enforcement of the civil rights legislation of the past three decades. Judicial scrutiny of employment and admissions practices on campuses has somewhat replaced the traditional judicial deference to academic decisions (Burnett and Matthews 1982). The legislation has often afforded potential plaintiffs in discrimination actions not only forums in which to be heard, but also realistic standards upon which to argue and remedies through which to be compensated. In other words, potential plaintiffs can get into court and have a real chance of winning and collecting damages. In much the same way, the rise of collective bargaining has increased outside involvement in internal campus affairs.

The number of federal and state regulations applicable to universities and colleges has increased markedly, and many of them involve outside scrutiny of some administrative decisions (V. Brown 1990; C. Greenleaf 1985); an example of enhanced regulation is in the area of access for people with disabilities. Finally, though nonjudicial in nature, external scrutiny and control have also increased, particularly for public institutions, with the rise of sometimes powerful coordinating boards for higher education in most states (V. Brown 1990).

Structural changes have also increased the involvement of colleges and universities in litigation. As the scale and complexity of individual institutions have increased, consensus has been more difficult to achieve and the courts have come to take a more active role in resolving the inevitable disputes (Kaplin and Lee 1995). Several factors have led to this state of affairs:

- Traditional processes of selection and acculturation have broken down as institutions have become more egalitarian and democratic and students and faculty have become increasingly diverse and demanding (Burnett and Matthews 1982).
- Given an increasing concern for reducing arbitrary decision making and recognizing constitutional and contractual rights, society has become more litigious, more frequently attempting to avail themselves of the courts to settle disputes (Burnett and Matthews 1982; Cloud 1992). The qualitative judgments that traditionally have been the hallmark of life in academe are exactly the type of decisions that have come to prompt litigation involving employment from faculty and legal challenges from students (C. Greenleaf 1985).
- The stakes in higher education have risen as the mobility of faculty has declined, providing incentives for disappointed faculty to vigorously challenge negative decisions about tenure and promotion instead of simply leaving for another institution. Similarly, students have come to expect more of institutions as costs have increased and employment markets tightened.
- Institutions have taken on a greater array of service functions over time—from increasing commitments to resi-

dence life to providing more counseling and remedial education—increasing the number of possible incidents giving rise to legal problems. In addition, students have come to expect more freedom in residence life, but institutions continue to be held legally responsible for their actions in many cases (C. Greenleaf 1985).

- Several new settings have emerged in higher education— community colleges, technical institutes, distance learning, international programs—and each has raised a distinctive set of legal issues.
- Both external regulations (e.g., regulation of human and animal subjects) and institutional self-regulation (e.g., formal grievance procedures) have increased, as have external demands for greater accountability. Institutions have also become more closely tied to the world outside academe through grants and other relationships with corporations and the federal government, and through direct federal aid.
- As institutions have adapted to various national and global trends—the technological revolution, internationalization, concerns about personal security—their position relative to the law has evolved accordingly.

Although higher education may not enjoy the same legal autonomy it once did, colleges and universities continue to enjoy great independence. Statutes and constitutions have delegated broad powers to colleges and universities, and institutions still have wide discretion to exercise those powers, provided they conform with the standards of public law, good faith, and individual rights (Leslie 1986). Under many circumstances, courts continue to defer to the judgment of academic institutions on academic decisions. They continue to recognize the uniqueness of higher education as well as the expertise of academic administrators in making decisions on academic matters (V. Brown 1990). After all, few other societal organizations have anything resembling professional peer review or voluntary accreditation. The change has come in the courts' willingness to actually hear and decide matters involving administrative discretion in academic matters.

The Distinction between Public and Private Institutions
Private and public institutions are treated differently under the law. Although private institutions have always been

chartered by the state and typically receive some public money, they have long been protected from certain types of governmental control. Nevertheless, the federal government in recent years has increasingly applied its regulations to private and public institutions alike.

Perhaps the main difference between private and public institutions is that private universities and colleges and their officers are not fully subject to the conditions of the U.S. Constitution. The Bill of Rights applies only to the state's acting against individuals, with the term "the state shall not . . ." recurring throughout the amendments. Public institutions are state actors and therefore are subject to the provisions.

The concept of state action determines whether courts will view a private institution as sufficiently "public" to make it subject to the provisions of the U.S. Constitution. In determining whether an action that is the subject of a complaint constitutes "state action," courts will assess whether a sufficiently close nexus exists between the state and the challenged action. In other words, can the action by a so-called private entity be as fairly treated as that of the state itself? State action exists when there is no practical distinction between the questioned action and something that is usually done by the government itself. Three approaches have emerged for attributing state action to an ostensibly private entity, such as a private college (Kaplin and Lee 1995). Actions become state action—and thus subject to constitutional constraints—when the private entity:

- Acts as an agent of government in performing a particular task delegated to it (the delegated powers theory);
- Performs a function that is generally considered to be the responsibility of the government (the public function theory); or
- Obtains substantial resources, prestige, or encouragement from its involvement with government (the government contacts theory).

Even though the U.S. Constitution does not apply to private institutions, other sources of individual rights resembling those in the Constitution are available to students and employees at private institutions. One is the antidiscrimination laws, which typically apply regardless of whether an institution accepts public money. Several of these statutes include provisions that allow for the recovery of damages by successful plaintiffs. Another potential source of protection is contract law. And a third source of individual rights can be found in many state constitutions, which often offer greater protection than the U.S. Constitution.

Many private institutions also are religious in nature, giving rise to potential First Amendment concerns. The First Amendment offers two protections to religious institutions: the Establishment Clause, which mandates that the state shall not sponsor any given religion, and the Free Exercise Clause, which prohibits the state from interfering with the practice of any religion. Neither clause is absolute. Religious universities and colleges can receive public support for nonreligious ends, such as building a residence hall or conducting scientific research, without offending the Establishment Clause. The three-part test for violation of that clause involves whether any governmental action has a secular legislative purpose, whether the action advances or inhibits religion (it should do neither), and whether the legislation fosters excessive governmental entanglement with religion (it should not) (Kaplin and Lee 1995). In certain situations, the government can deny federal support, particularly to institutions that discriminate, without encountering a problem with the Free Exercise Clause. For example, the decision of the U.S. Supreme Court in *Bob Jones University v. United States* (1983) upheld the denial of federal government funding to an institution based on its racially restrictive policies on dating and marriage, even though the policies were based on religious doctrine.

The Attorney-Client Relationship
Three principal models exist for organizing the provision of legal services at colleges and universities (Kaplin and Lee 1995). The first is in-house counsel. Larger private institutions, as well as some public ones, often retain a staff of lawyers who perform general legal work for the institution and delegate more specialized or complex work to law firms that work under the general oversight of the campus counsel (Bickel 1994). The second, often seen at smaller schools, is for the institution to retain a law firm that specializes in higher education law to represent it. The third, involving public institutions, includes arrangements with systemwide attorneys or the education division of the state attorney general's office to provide legal counsel (Roster and Woodward 1996).

The roles of university counsel are varied; they serve as:

- Adviser-counselor, participating on committees and councils to guide administrative decisions clear of potential legal problems;
- Educator-mediator, explaining legal procedures and requirements to often disagreeing members of the university community;
- Manager-administrator, managing professional and support staff and directing the operations of the office and activities of outside counsel;
- Drafter of documents and reviewer of documents drafted by others;
- Litigator in a variety of adjudicatory venues, both on and off campus; and
- Spokesperson to regulatory agencies, accrediting associations, and the media on legal matters involving the university (Daane 1985).

In these multiple roles, institutions should have several expectations of counsel: loyalty to the institution, familiarity with the special nature of academic institutions, full participation in campus policy-making councils, service as the conscience of the institution, skepticism when the administration reviews major issues, and the anticipation and resolution of conflicts that arise (O'Neil 1993). It is important to remember, however, that counsel serve in more of an advisory role than one focused on making policy decisions (Bickel 1994).

Another basic expectation of all attorneys is that information communicated to them by any client will remain confidential. The attorney-client privilege forbids an attorney from knowingly revealing to anyone information exchanged in the course of representing a client. It also prevents anyone from compelling the attorney to reveal the information during discovery within the context of litigation. The same protections apply to any material that the attorney produces related to the representation of a client. The exception to the general rule of confidentiality is when it is the client's intention to commit a serious crime or fraudulent act and disseminating the information is necessary to prevent violation of the law (Drinan 1993).

One complication in the attorney-client relationship at colleges or universities is that it is not always clear who is the client (Bickel 1994; O'Neil 1993). Often, counsel may serve several clients concurrently: the governing board, the state attorney general, the administration, the faculty, nonadministrative persons or groups, groups associated with the institution (independent alumni groups, for example), and the legal profession itself. Even though university attorneys serve all of these groups, counsel typically opt to represent the interests closest to the entity employing them, whether that entity is the institution, the system, or the state. For instance, in a dispute between the president and the board, the attorney would typically serve the board and inform the president accordingly. The president would then need to retain independent outside counsel. Similarly, were a faculty member to be involved in a conflict with the administration—whether the central administration or a dean or chair—campus counsel would represent the administration.

Therefore, the general rule is that when the interests of the institution oppose those of an individual staff member, faculty member, or administrator (including deans and chairs), counsel retained by the university will likely remain loyal to the institution and the individual should seek counsel other than that provided by the institution. When university counsel anticipate or recognize such a situation, it is both inappropriate and imprudent for him or her to advise the individual involved. When an attorney has been involved on multiple sides of an issue, the resulting conflict of interest often disqualifies him or her from serving any side.

For example, suppose a department chair, fearful of an adverse personnel matter, contacts a university attorney, who has already conferred with the president, provost, or dean about the matter. The attorney can only suggest that the chair retain personal counsel (O'Neil 1993). Even if the attorney is unaware of the matter at the time of the call, the sensible response is to strongly discourage the chair from sharing any information with him or her, as any communication between counsel and a later adversary might create a conflict of interest or a problem of confidentiality. The bottom line is that counsel can advise only one side in a dispute involving multiple institutional actors and that side may not always be the dean of the school or the department chair (O'Neil 1993). The actor farthest removed from the locus of control at the institution should seek personal counsel in disputes with the institution.

For example, suppose a department chair, fearful of an adverse personnel matter, contacts a university attorney, who has already conferred with the president, provost, or dean about the matter.

In addition to the problem of determining where institutional counsel owe their loyalty, several possible situations could represent ethical dilemmas for campus counsel:

- Campus counsel may be assigned a project that they know violates the Constitution or another law, say drafting a policy aimed at curbing free expression on campus.
- The lawyer may be asked to take an indefensible position in negotiations or litigation.
- Sometimes the advice of counsel is disregarded, circumvented, or misused, as, for example, when a client, disregarding the advice of counsel, resists accepting a sound offer of settlement in pending litigation or decides to make a premature or unsound settlement.
- An institution receives advice from shadow counsel that conflicts with that of the university's attorney (O'Neil 1993).

In such situations, counsel often must confront ethical issues by performing the duties assigned after stating their objections, although they have little recourse short of resignation.

Pretrial and Trial Procedures
A plaintiff takes the first of many procedural steps in a lawsuit by filing a complaint against the defendant. The complaint describes the facts of the situation at issue and proposes a set of remedies to be imposed upon the defendant by the court. The plaintiff not only must file the complaint with the court, but also must serve the complaint upon the defendant or defendants in the action. The defendant then has a specified number of days to respond by filing a document called an "answer." As a representative of the institution, an academic administrator may be served with a complaint from a plaintiff. The document is time sensitive and should be forwarded to the institution's counsel immediately.

Attached to the answer may be a motion for summary judgment. At any point in the pretrial process, and often before it even begins, the defendant can file a motion for summary judgment. In the motion, the defendant concedes that even if the facts the plaintiff alleges are true, the plaintiff has not stated a valid claim that would entitle him or her to relief. In other words, no genuine issue of material fact remains, and the law as applied to the remaining facts entitles the defendant to relief. If no summary judgment is issued, the action proceeds to trial at the conclusion of the set pretrial discovery period. Moreover, the defendant may also file a cross-complaint, bringing an action against the plaintiff under the same set of facts.

A potential plaintiff will be denied access to any court that does not have jurisdiction over either the subject matter of the lawsuit (subject matter jurisdiction) or the person who is the subject of the action (personal jurisdiction) (Kaplin and Lee 1995). Questions of jurisdiction are different in federal and state courts. Federal courts have jurisdiction over federal questions—issues of federal statutory or constitutional law— as well as diversity actions (between citizens of different states). State courts can hear most of what is brought before them, even matters from another state, assuming no provision exists for exclusive federal jurisdiction over a matter (as in controversies between two states). When appropriate, a defendant in a state court action can petition the court to remove appropriate cases to federal court. Under the doctrine articulated in *United Mine Workers v. Gibbs* (1966), federal courts may hear state questions of law along with federal cases before them if both cases "derive from a common nucleus of operative fact"—that is, the two actions arise out of the same facts—and are normally the type of issues heard together. Nevertheless, a federal court may decline to hear a state law claim it if is a novel or complex question of state law or if the state claim substantially predominates over the federal claim.

Personal jurisdiction differs from subject matter jurisdiction. The theory underlying personal jurisdiction is that courts have jurisdiction only over defendants who reside in a state, commit torts or conduct business there, or consent to be sued there. Personal jurisdiction would likely attach to visiting faculty from another state working at a university or out-of-state students attending classes there. "Long-arm" statutes determine whether courts have personal jurisdiction over nonresidents. Under the decision in *Worldwide Volkswagen Corp. v. Woodson* (1980), long-arm jurisdiction is based on whether the defendant has "minimum contacts" with the state.

Even if there are no jurisdictional issues that prevent access to court, several other situations may cause a court not to hear a case (Kaplin and Lee 1995):

- Under the abstention doctrine, a federal court will refuse to hear a case so that a state court can instead decide the case to resolve issues of state law.
- "Standing" is the concept that one needs to be the actual aggrieved party in order to bring a lawsuit. A variation on the requirement for standing is class action litigation. A class action involves a large group of litigants having common characteristics who band together under the representation of a single attorney or law firm to attempt to redress a situation typical among them.
- Mootness—when the passage of time or a change in events causes a matter to no longer be a controversy—is another barrier to access. For instance, in an action brought by a student challenging a determination by an institution about some academic requirement for graduation, the student's actual graduation would render the case moot.
- A statute of limitation might also prevent access. Statutes of limitation place time limits on when a plaintiff may bring an action. They are different in different states and for different kinds of action, though contract issues often have a six-year limit and tort cases typically have a three-year limit. Statutes of limitation usually run from when a claim first accrues or when the potential plaintiff should have first noticed the claim, whichever circumstance is more reasonable. Certain mechanisms are available to delay the statute's running (called "tolling") when it is reasonable to impose them.
- All internal administrative remedies should be exhausted before a court will allow a plaintiff to bring a lawsuit, but courts will make an exception to the exhaustion of remedies principle when the administrative procedures appear to be stacked against the plaintiff so as to render the procedure a waste of time. For instance, if the university has administrative procedures available regarding a certain type of issue, the plaintiff must exhaust them before pursuing remedies in the courts. If, however, the plaintiff would not receive a fair hearing under the procedures available, then he or she is allowed to move directly to court.

Once the plaintiff has access to court, discovery ensues. Discovery is the collection of information by the various sides involved in an action to clarify the facts and legal issues involved. The basic principle in discovery is that it extends to any matter that is relevant and not privileged. The rules of civil procedure that structure the discovery process to favor litigants' broad and honest sharing of information also have mechanisms to punish those who do not act in accordance with the intended letter and spirit of the process.

Three principal means are available to collect information during discovery—depositions, interrogatories, and document requests. Depositions are question-and-answer sessions between attorneys and those thought to have relevant information about the particulars of the case. They are adversarial in nature—all opposing counsel have the right to examine the witness—and are recorded and transcribed by a court stenographer. Interrogatories consist of written questions from counsel for one side in the litigation to parties on the other side. When either side employs expert witnesses, opposing counsel question them through interrogatories and may also choose to take their depositions based on their responses. Document requests, often attached to interrogatories, are a vehicle to bring relevant files and other materials to the attention of opposing counsel.

In a hypothetical action challenging a negative decision about tenure on the basis of discrimination against gender, the plaintiff might request depositions (or compel them through a subpoena, if necessary) from various administrators involved in the tenure process, members of the unit's and the institution's tenure committees, and outside experts on tenure and gender discrimination. Interrogatories might be directed toward individuals who could assist in locating relevant information in the case, such as the types of files that are kept for tenure applications, and document requests might seek production of the contents of those files. The defense might also offer expert witnesses and would seek their depositions along with that of the plaintiff.

Conferences between clients and counsel are an example of the less formal aspects of the discovery process. The attorney-client privilege precludes information exchanged during these discussions from being available to the opposing side through discovery. Any material produced by counsel in the context of the attorney-client relationship (called "attorney work product") is also privileged. Both plaintiffs and defendants use the attorney-client privilege, the attorney work product privilege, or other recognized privileges (physician-patient, for instance) to seek to limit the evidence to be admitted at trial. In other words, counsel claim privilege to prevent the production of information or documents as potential evidence that can be used at trial. The device used to make these requests to the court to exclude evidence is called a motion *in limine.*

Before trial, a court-mandated mediation conference generally is held to encourage settlement out of court. At any point in the litigation, it is possible that some or all of the litigants will enter into a voluntary settlement agreement. At that point, a document called a "decree" is filed with the court, thus disposing of the litigation. Settlements often involve monetary compensation to the plaintiff and an agreement that the settlement acts to dispose of all potential future claims. Sometimes a stipulation compelling the sides to keep the terms of the settlement confidential is included in the agreement. In the interests of clearing crowded court dockets and saving taxpayers' and litigants' money, judges typically push the sides in a lawsuit toward settling claims.

At the end of a case—after the court has been presented with the evidence collected by both sides and has considered their arguments in the context of the relevant law—the court renders a final judgment. The judgment either dismisses the case or fashions a remedy. After the final judgment, the losing party may file an appeal within the typically short time set by the court rules of the jurisdiction. After that date, the losing side forfeits all subsequent rights to appeal the decision. Moreover, the losers cannot simply relitigate the same case in a different court. The concept of *res judicata* (also known as "claim preclusion") dictates that claims already litigated cannot be heard again. Nor can the losing party try to bring the same action in a different state. The Full Faith and Credit Clause of the U.S. Constitution requires courts to give the same credit to decisions rendered in another state that it gives to ones in their own state.

The judgment in a case will include one of three types of remedies, and the court can choose any one or a combination:

- *Money damages* include *compensatory damages* intended to compensate the plaintiff for actual damage suffered as a result of the defendant's actions. *Punitive damages* are intended to go beyond "making whole" the injury to the plaintiff through compensatory damages and punish the defendant.

- *Injunctive relief* is an order from the court compelling the defendant to do something *(mandatory injunction)* or not to do something *(prohibitory injunction)*. Injunctions can be temporary or permanent. Courts will hear petitions for temporary injunctions as soon as possible, given their usual emergency nature, and will issue the injunction if the plaintiff is likely to prevail on the merits of the action when eventually seeking a permanent injunction.

- *Attorney's fees* are available in certain situations, such as frivolous lawsuits, and are mandated by statute under the civil rights laws.

If one does not comply with the relief the court orders, he or she can be held in contempt and may be imprisoned or fined as punishment or until coerced into compliance.

Individual or Institutional Liability: Authority and Delegation

Trustees, officers, and administrators at colleges and universities can take only those actions or make only those decisions for which they have the authority if they wish to avoid personal liability. Authority derives from different sources at public and private institutions, but ultimate authority at any institution is vested in its governing board. Governing boards obtain authority directly from the people of a given state, through the legislature via statute at public institutions (or through state constitution for a few institutions) and through charters and articles of incorporation at private schools (Cloud 1992). These boards—called trustees, regents, visitors, curators, or the like—have duties analogous to corporate boards of directors. They are responsible for overseeing the overall functioning of the university, not the details of its daily operation.

Because the board has ultimate authority for the operation of the institution, it is often the entity against which plaintiffs bring lawsuits. Individual board members, however, are shielded from personal liability when institutions are held to be responsible to plaintiffs if there is no:

- Manifest mismanagement (gross negligence, more than mistakes of judgment);

- Nonmanagement (failure to acquire the information necessary to supervise, or failure to attend meetings where policies are considered); or
- Self-dealing (failure to fully disclose major potential conflicts of interest and unfairness to the institution in a transaction marked by self-interest) (Kaplin and Lee 1995; Moots 1991).

Officers and administrators at institutions need authority to act; they derive their authority by delegation from the institution's governing board. One of the board's most important tasks is to appoint a chief executive officer, typically called a president or chancellor. The president or chancellor is charged with organizing and operating the university, including employing administrators, staff, and faculty. Officials and administrators at public institutions typically derive their authority from state administrative procedure acts, state coordinating board regulations, and court decisions. For the institution, authority is delegated through job descriptions and operational procedures (Cloud 1992). As with boards, those employed by the institution are indemnified against personal liability for actions taken within their authority. If one does not have authority to take a particular action in the name of the university, he or she is open to personal liability—whether in a case grounded in negligence, contract, or constitutional issues—unless the issue of authority is resolved.

Four types of authority are possible:

- *Express authority* is found within the plain meaning of the grant of authority.
- *Implied authority* is inferred from express authority as being necessary for actually exercising express authority. In essence, implied authority fills in the gaps in actual authority. Because every situation that might arise in the course of a job cannot be anticipated and expressly addressed in a job description, implied authority covers what is reasonable and necessary for administrators and others to exercise their express authority daily.
- *Apparent authority* is the case in which one has no actual authority but induces the reasonable belief in another person that he or she does.
- *Inherent authority* involves implied powers when written words would not be sensible, such as the power to main-

tain proper order, decorum, or discipline over students (Cloud 1992; Kaplin and Lee 1995).

Courts construe authority considering all sources of law—particularly the common law, contracts, institutional rules and regulations, and custom and usage at an institution—in determining whether an individual officer or administrator has acted within his or her authority and thus should be shielded from personal liability.

Even if an officer or administrator exceeds his or her authority, the act may be made valid under certain circumstances, allowing him or her to escape potential personal liability for the consequences of the action—for example, if the unauthorized act is subsequently ratified by the governing board or in the event of estoppel, which imputes authority for an action when necessary to protect a plaintiff who acted in reasonable reliance on the unauthorized act. In other words, courts will not allow someone to escape liability to a plaintiff who acted in reasonable reliance on a given representation simply because the person making the representation lacked authority.

When confronted with tort actions against them, institutions may also have available traditional defenses such as governmental immunity and tort claims acts (public institutions) and charitable immunity (private institutions). Governmental immunity protects only institutions and does not protect an administrator sued in an individual capacity, but administrators will likely be protected under the doctrine of official immunity if found to be acting within their authority in performing a discretionary duty.

Finally, the Eleventh Amendment to the U.S. Constitution may also provide protection against liability in some cases. The Eleventh Amendment asserts that states cannot be sued for money damages in federal courts (although they can in state courts) unless the state has waived immunity. Public officials—including certain college and university boards and administrators—sued in their official capacity sometimes benefit from Eleventh Amendment protection. Whether or not an official is protected is a matter of whether or not a public institution is seen as a state entity, that is, whether it is an "alter ego" of the state operated by administrators who are "state" officials. Often, community college officials are not considered alter egos of the state, because community colleges are governed by locally elected boards and raise revenue through local tax districts (Cloud 1992; Julian 1995). Whether increasing support from nongovernmental sources at state-aided institutions will be sufficient to break the alter ego connection remains an open question (Julian 1995). Another important exception to Eleventh Amendment protection is the case when plaintiffs' constitutional rights have been violated by state officials. Federal courts will hear such cases and will allow plaintiffs to sue officials as individuals in certain acts of discrimination. Officials can then be held personally liable for monetary damages for intentional violations of these constitutional rights (Cloud 1992; Julian 1995).

THE EMPLOYMENT RELATIONSHIP
WITH FACULTY AND STAFF

The essence of the relationship between employers and employees is the employment contract, whether within the context of one-on-one bargaining between the parties or as part of a collective bargaining agreement. Closely related to the employment contract are decisions about hiring and promotion, each of which raises issues of equal protection and due process, given constitutional provisions and statutory protections under the antidiscrimination laws. These same issues commonly arise in decisions about reappointment, tenure, and promotion, as well as in the setting of the dismissal and retirement of tenured faculty and other employees. In addition, affirmative action frequently intersects with the employment relationship.

Academic administrators must keep in mind several very practical concerns in decisions about hiring and promotion, including avoiding inappropriate questions during interviews, respecting an individual's right to privacy, and following the immigration laws. Deans and chairs must also understand and respect faculty members' right of academic freedom, while at the same time evaluating faculty performance and taking action when it is insufficient, and investigating and perhaps punishing employee misconduct such as sexual harassment.

Foundations of the Relationship between Employer and Employee
Contractual relationships

Employment relationships between institutions and employees are contractual in nature. The core of the employment contract is the express terminology contained in some formal communication, whether a simple appointment letter or something more complicated (Moll 1995). The actual contract involves much more than formal writing, however (Kaplin and Lee 1995). At public institutions, certain state statutes and administrative regulations are understood to be part of the contract. For example, a state statute covering tenure is viewed as an addition to the contract and supersedes portions of the contract that conflict with it.

Other documents may be incorporated into the contract. For instance, the contract is read to incorporate an employee handbook, if one exists (D. Duffy 1995). Similarly, the collected rules and regulations of an institution—if the institution has adopted the American Association of University Professors's (AAUP's) 1940 Statement of Principles governing tenure, for instance—become part of the employment contract by implication. In fact, the employment contract often consists of an appointment letter with specific reference to an employee handbook and the institution's rules and regulations (Moll 1995). Regardless of the form of the employment contract, it should refer to such issues as duration of employment; rank, promotion, and tenure; duties and responsibilities; salary and benefits; handbooks and policy manuals; renewal of appointment; and termination or dismissal (Moll 1995).

Any informational gaps in an employment contract are filled either by some evidence of the intent of the parties or through reference to academic custom and usage (Kaplin and Lee 1995). Evidence of intent may include written or unwritten statements made at the time of hiring. Academic custom and usage are the usual practices of an institution, whether they are contained in official documents like faculty handbooks or are simply common understandings and routines on campus. Custom and usage can only fill gaps, however; it cannot contradict contract terms. In addition, in implying and interpreting contract terms, courts will use the common law of a given state. In other words, all of the decisions over time on contract cases in that jurisdiction will be used to construe the contract (Kaplin and Lee 1995).

Once agreed upon, a contract can be changed or voided in several ways. One is through recession. A contract is treated as though it never existed when there is fraud in the inducement (Kaplin and Lee 1995), that is, when the terms or other aspects of the contractual relationship are misrepresented in a way that leads someone to agree to enter into the agreement with a false impression of the risks, duties, or obligations undertaken. Contracts may also include prohibitions on certain conduct—such as amorous relationships between faculty and current students—and violations may be grounds for canceling the contract. At religious institutions, restrictions on the personal conduct of employees based on church doctrine may be included in contracts and provide grounds for cancellation. In addition, the right to amend a contract can be reserved by one or both parties, and thus a contract can be amended with the mutual consent of the contracting parties. A contract can be waived in the same way (Kaplin and Lee 1995).

Different types of contractual relationships often exist when different types of employees or different types of institutions are involved. In the case of faculty, for instance, part-time and probationary faculty are commonly treated differently from tenured faculty. Sometimes, because of the religion clauses in the First Amendment, faculty at religious institutions may be limited in the recourse to courts because of an unwillingness to concur with church doctrine.

Collective bargaining

Certain employment contracts are a product of collective bargaining. Collective bargaining is a procedure directed toward reaching collective agreements between employers and accredited representatives of unionized employees concerning the conditions of employment, including compensation. The rules of collective bargaining, outlined in the National Labor Relations Act, require that the sides in a given negotiation deal with each other in an open and fair manner and sincerely endeavor to overcome obstacles to an agreement, even though they are in a bilateral and adversarial relationship (McHugh 1973; Schwartzman 1973).

The basis of collective bargaining is the bargaining unit. The National Labor Relations Board will recognize a bargaining unit that represents a "community of interest"—a group of people with similar situations and interests—and has been approved by majority vote in an election. Universities can voluntarily recognize a bargaining unit or the group can petition the NLRB for a certification election. In collective bargaining, the community of interest is represented in contract negotiations exclusively by its elected representatives (McHugh 1973; Schwartzman 1973). After a union is certified, union membership can be compelled and dues collected, including through payroll deductions (Olswang 1988).

As personnel who serve primarily in a managerial function, deans and chairs are not typically considered employees within the context of collective bargaining. Instead, they are considered to be supervisors. Faculty are commonly not seen as managerial and can form a bargaining unit if they so desire. A notable exception to the general rule is the decision in *NLRB v. Yeshiva University* (1980), where faculty were found to be heavily involved in administration and governance and were thus held to have interests that coincided with administrators (Julius 1993b; Lee and Begin 1983–84). The *Yeshiva* ruling applies only to "Yeshiva-type" institutions, where faculty have a substantial role in administrative decision making. Still, although *Yeshiva* is an exception to the general rule, the decision has been used to exclude faculty at private colleges from bargaining.

At private institutions, collective bargaining is subject to federal law, particularly the National Labor Relations Act and the Wagner and Taft-Hartley Acts, if the conduct at issue is deemed to have a significant effect on interstate commerce (which most private institutions have) (Schwartzman 1973). In the case of religious institutions, the collective bargaining statutes apply where the institution has become "secularized" but are not applicable when there is risk of entanglement with an institution's "religious missions," pursuant to the Establishment Clause of the First Amendment. In fact, NLRB jurisdiction will likely be denied at church-related institutions where faculty and staff can be dismissed for religious reasons because of the risk of excessive governmental entanglement with religion (Franke and Mintz 1987).

Public institutions are subject to state labor laws, which are often more restrictive than federal law (a more limited right to strike, for instance). State agencies often fill gaps in their collective bargaining statutes by reference to federal law (Kaplin and Lee 1995). And federal antidiscrimination laws apply to both management and labor in a collective bargaining negotiation.

When parties in collective bargaining are unable to reach an agreement or when a question of interpretation arises, several techniques for resolution are available. The most extreme is the strike, which is typically more limited for public employees than for employees of private institutions. Short of calling a strike, labor may also file an unfair labor practices claim with the NLRB. An impasse might also result in management's imposition of its "last, best offer." More commonly, mediation or arbitration occurs under the direction of a neutral third party (McHugh 1973).

Hiring and Promotion Decisions: Equal Protection and Due Process
Constitutional and statutory protection

Employment decisions based not on individual qualifications or merit but on immutable characteristics—race, national origin, gender, disability, age, religion—are discriminatory under the U.S. Constitution, state constitutions, and federal and state legislation. Several of these categories are protected by Title VII or other federal antidiscrimination statutes, as well as by the Equal Protection Clause of the Fourteenth Amendment, when public institutions are involved. Discrimination cases brought against public institutions on constitutional grounds are afforded the highest judicial scrutiny. Thus, the accused state actor must have a compelling state interest to justify the discrimination. Discrimination on the basis of sexual orientation is considered by courts under a more permissive standard—the government has a rational basis for its actions—making these cases much more difficult to prove for plaintiffs. Approximately one dozen states have included sexual orientation as a protected category in their state antidiscrimination laws, however.

In an employment discrimination case brought under one of the several federal antidiscrimination statutes, the plaintiff does not prove that the defendant discriminated but that the explanation offered by the defendant for the employment decision is untrue (Kaplin and Lee 1995). In a discrimination case, the plaintiff must present sufficient evidence to raise an inference of discrimination, which the defendant then rebuts by presenting evidence of a legitimate nondiscriminatory reason for the action alleged to be discriminatory. The plaintiff then has the opportunity to prove that the defendant's reason is a pretext and unworthy of belief (Grexa 1992; Hagen and Hagen 1995; Kaplin and Lee 1995; Swedlow 1994).

The Equal Employment Opportunity Commission is charged with investigating discrimination complaints and has broad powers to collect evidence, including subpoena power (Grexa 1992). Discrimination claims are difficult to prove in academe, particularly for faculty, given the subjective nature of their positions (Kaplin and Lee 1995)—for instance, the necessity to prove unequal treatment of otherwise similar individuals in order to win where such individuals are likely to be difficult to identify, particularly on a given faculty. In addition, performance standards often shift over time, and comparisons of faculty productivity and assessments of quality across disciplines, for instance, are difficult to make.

Several statutes apply to employment discrimination in both public and private institutions. The basic principle underlying the antidiscrimination statutes is the Equal Protection

Discrimination claims are difficult to prove in academe, particularly for faculty, given the subjective nature of their positions.

provision of the Fourteenth Amendment. In its essence, equal protection is the idea that different people should not be treated differently based on their membership in a particular group, absent a very good reason to do so, such as religious principle or affirmative action. Although the Equal Protection Clause offers somewhat parallel protections to the federal statutes, it is more limited in several respects. In particular, the Equal Protection Clause typically:

- Has more stringent standards than the antidiscrimination laws, usually requiring intentional discrimination;
- Usually does not apply to private institutions; and
- Lacks the enforcement mechanisms that exist in the statutes (Kaplin and Lee 1995).

Title VII, Title IX, and Section 1981. Title VII covers discrimination based on race, national origin, gender, or religion. Two types of Title VII claims can be made: disparate treatment and disparate impact. *Disparate treatment* is the situation in which someone is treated less favorably because of an immutable characteristic; thus, the employer intended to discriminate against the plaintiff. The only exception to Title VII disparate treatment is if discrimination occurs within the context of a bona fine occupational qualification (Araujo 1996). For instance, a court might hold discrimination on the basis of religion to be permissible if religion is an essential part of the job, as with a professor of theology at a church-related institution. At the same institution, however, an employee in a non-ministerial function—the campus director of public safety, for instance—would not be within the exception for bona fide occupational qualification. Finally, another law, the Equal Pay Act, addresses discrimination in salaries and issues of comparable worth (equal pay for equal work), a classic situation involving disparate treatment. Actions under the act are generally unsuccessful, however (Kaplin and Lee 1995).

Disparate impact is the situation when an ostensibly neutral policy turns out to be discriminatory (Hagen and Hagen 1995). In other words, an employment policy that seems neutral on its face might violate Title VII, regardless of the intent of the employer, if it has a significantly disparate impact on a protected group (Redlich 1992). The institution can justify the use of such a policy if it can prove that the criteria have a manifest relationship to job performance and if a significant academic interest justifies the use of the criteria (Redlich 1992). Disparate impact cases often involve attempts by plaintiffs to establish, through statistical evidence, that an employment selection technique or administrative system produced a disparate impact on a particular group (James, Gomez, and Bulgar 1995). Disparate impact cases may be brought as class actions.

Despite the traditional stance of the judiciary toward higher education, the trend has been away from the doctrine of academic abstention in these types of cases (Kaplin and Lee 1995; Pacholski 1992). If an employer is found to have intentionally engaged in unlawful employment practices, courts have undertaken the responsibility to fashion a set of remedies. The theory underlying remedies is to make the victim whole, to the extent possible. In other words, the remedy should place the victim in the situation he or she would have occupied had the wrong not occurred (Pacholski 1992). Remedies might include an injunction against future discriminatory behavior. They might also include compensatory and punitive damages, such as back pay and attorneys' fees (Pacholski 1992). In the case of a dismissal, reinstatement is a common remedy. It is uncommon, however, that a remedy would involve the granting of tenure, unless it were clear to the court that the institution would not fairly consider the application for tenure (Kaplin and Lee 1995; Pacholski 1992).

Title IX addresses discrimination at public and private institutions that receive federal funds. Like Title VII, Title IX contains an exemption for discrimination based on religious principle. Actions under Title IX offer plaintiffs an advantage over Title VII, because Title IX has no cap for damages. In addition, the statute of limitation under Title IX is often more favorable than under Title VII. Instead of the 180-day statute under Title VII, the statute in Title IX actions is borrowed from the state where the action is brought.

Section 1981 (42 U.S.C. 1981) addresses racial discrimination against people of all races, as well as discrimination on the basis of national origin where race is intertwined. The statute is applicable to both public and private institutions. Section 1981 overlaps with Title VII in coverage, but it allows for more extensive remedies and a longer statute of limitation than Title VII (Kaplin and Lee 1995).

Americans with Disabilities Act. The ADA prohibits discrimination on the basis of disability against a disabled person who is otherwise qualified for a position. The statute also requires that institutions ensure equal access to opportunities and services to persons with disabilities by making necessary "reasonable accommodations" that can be achieved without "undue hardship" to the institution (Drimmer 1993; Raines and Rossow 1994). The act expands the protection afforded by its direct predecessor, Section 504 of the Rehabilitation Act, and is enforced by the federal EEOC (Drimmer 1993; Haggard 1993). The ADA has broad definitions of what is "reasonable accommodation," who is a "qualified individual," and what constitutes a "disability" (S. Adler 1994).

Under the ADA, reasonable accommodation in the context of employment is determined case by case based on what is needed to allow persons with disabilities to perform a job while not imposing an undue burden on employers (S. Adler 1994; Duston, Russell, and Kerr 1992, 1993; Johnson 1993; Rothstein 1991). The ADA will allow institutions to avoid making necessary accommodations only when the expenses associated with accommodations are excessive in the context of the resources and nature of the institution and thus are not reasonable (S. Adler 1994; Raines and Rossow 1994). Illustrations of reasonable accommodations that employers must provide include making existing facilities accessible to applicants and employees, modifying work schedules, reassigning someone to a vacant position, acquiring or modifying equipment or devices, appropriately adjusting or modifying examinations, and providing qualified readers or interpreters (S. Adler 1994). Once again, the judgment about whether a type of accommodation is reasonable depends on the case.

Disabled individuals qualify for protection under the ADA only if they meet the essential eligibility requirements for a position and the essential functions in it (Duston, Russell, and Kerr 1992, 1993; M. Edwards 1992–93; Haggard 1993; Raines and Rossow 1994; Rothstein 1991). Examples of evidence of essential functions of the job include job descriptions written in anticipation of posting a position, collective bargaining agreements, experience of others in the job, and the consequences to the employer of not having a specific portion of a job performed (S. Adler 1994; M. Edwards 1992–93). Given the importance of job descriptions in determining eligibility for a position, employers should take care in listing essential functions and not focus on functions that are marginal to the execution of the job (Duston, Russell, and Kerr 1992, 1993). A classic example of an individual's being found not qualified for the essential functions of a position, even with reasonable accommodations, is Southeastern Community College v. Davis (1979), in which a hearing-impaired nursing student was disqualified from a degree program for safety reasons (Rothstein 1991).

A disabled person is defined under the ADA as an individual with a physical or mental impairment that substantially limits one or more major life activities, an individual with a record or known history of such physical or mental impairment, or an individual whom others regard as having such an impairment (M. Edwards 1992–93). Contagious and noncontagious diseases, including HIV, qualify as disabilities under the ADA. The same is true of alcoholism (M. Edwards 1992–93; Haggard 1993; Heinemann 1995; Raines and Rossow 1994; Taylor 1995). Mental impairments included under the ADA, like under the Rehabilitation Act that preceded it, are broad and currently include, among others, schizophrenia, bipolar disorder, post-traumatic stress disorder, and borderline personality disorder. Other specific disorders are presently excluded, however, particularly sexual behavior disorders, compulsive gambling, kleptomania, pyromania, and certain substance use disorders (such as the use of illegal drugs) (M. Edwards 1992–93; Haggard 1993). The EEOC also currently excludes from the definition of impairment certain environmental, cultural, or economic disadvantages, such as poverty, lack of education, or a prison record. Similarly, neither advanced age nor gender identity disorders are now defined as impairments (M. Edwards 1992–93).

Even under these broad definitions of reasonable accommodation, qualified individual, and disability, however, disabled individuals, including those with mental disabilities, still must be able to perform the essentials of a given job (Taylor 1995). For example, the difficulties in learning, comprehension, social interaction, and behavior that might be present in an individual classified as mentally retarded could substantially and unreasonably impede performance of a job (Haggard 1993). Courts increasingly are holding all employees to performance standards, irrespective of their disabilities (Lee and Ruger 1997), provided that the employer makes reasonable accommodations and acts in good faith (M. Edwards 1992–93; Haggard 1993). Still, the definition of employment discrimination on the basis of disability includes the creation of a work environment that is so oppressive and intolerable that the employee has no choice but to resign (Johnson 1993).

Under the ADA, employers are not allowed to question applicants directly about disabilities, nor are medical or psychological examinations permitted until after an offer of employment has been extended to a job candidate (Duston, Russell, and Kerr 1992, 1993; James, Gomez, and Bulgar 1995; Taylor 1995). Examinations for HIV are permitted only if exposure would pose a direct threat to the health and safety of others and only if all persons in a job classification are tested, as in the case of a health care worker who performs invasive procedures (Heinemann 1995). Typical faculty or administrative duties in an academic setting likely do not pose a sufficient threat to merit testing employees performing these functions. The bottom line is that employers may ask questions directed at learning whether a candidate is capable of doing a particular job but may not ask questions directly related to determining whether the candidate has a disability. For example, questions about past treatment for drug abuse or history of nervous breakdown are not permitted (M. Edwards 1992–93; Heinemann 1995). These same prohibitions extend to background checks (Duston, Russell, and Kerr 1992, 1993).

Therefore, in deciding whether to hire a candidate for a position, institutions may legitimately refuse to hire any person with a disability who:

- Lacks the minimum qualifications for the job;
- Is unable to perform the job's essential functions;
- Requires an accommodation that would be an undue hardship;
- Would pose a direct threat to the health or safety of the individual or others;
- Is less qualified than other applicants; and
- Fails to meet any other criteria that are job related and consistent with what is necessary to operate an institution (Duston, Russell, and Kerr 1992, 1993).

Moreover, the ADA does not require affirmative action in hiring or employment. No affirmative obligation exists to make reasonable accommodations to qualified individuals with disabilities, only a prohibition against discrimination against those persons with disabilities who can perform the essential functions of a position with or without reasonable accommodations (Duston, Russell, and Kerr 1992, 1993).

Age Discrimination in Employment Act. The ADEA covers discrimination in employment because of age, an area omitted under Title VII (Carkeek et al. 1988). The act covers not only discrimination in actual employment, but also discrimination in requirements to receive benefits and incentives for retirement (DiGiovanni 1989, 1993a, 1993b). The ADEA requires that older workers receive benefits equivalent to those afforded younger workers (Loren 1992), but the principle does not apply to voluntary early retirement plans, which must remain strictly voluntary and free of coercion by the employer (DiGiovanni 1993a, 1993b; Loren 1992; Stith and Kohlburn 1992). Because incentives for retirement are typically offered during only a short window of opportunity and are not usually available to employees discharged involuntarily, the possibility for coercion is real (Harper 1993). Moreover, mandatory retirement for faculty is no longer permitted, and policies against rehiring retired faculty based on age are suspect (Kaplin and Lee 1995; Ruebhausen 1988).

Individuals who believe they are a victim of discrimination because of their age have 180 days (or 300 days in states with appropriate agencies for investigating claims) from the time the employee receives notice of the alleged act of discrimination to file a claim with the EEOC, which then investigates (unless an appropriate state agency exists). The individual has two years from the date of the violation to initiate a lawsuit in federal or state court (three years if the allegedly discriminatory act is willful). An age limit is no longer imposed on who can bring an action under the statute (Kaplin and Lee 1995).

Litigants have long had the right to a trial by jury under the ADEA, a factor that has led to generally greater success and higher awards than for other victims of bias. (With the 1990 Civil Rights Act, jury trials are now available in both Title VII and ADA actions.) Remedies under the ADEA include back pay and benefits, as well as liquidated damages equal to double the back pay in cases of willful violations (DiGiovanni 1989, 1993a, 1993b). And, as under the other legislation that addresses discrimination in employment, the employee wins by proving that the employer's stated non-discriminatory reason for the alleged discriminatory act is false (DiGiovanni 1989, 1993a, 1993b).

Deans and chairs can adopt preventive measures against discrimination based on age in employment practices on campus. These measures apply equally to other types of discrimination.

- Employment evaluations typically include documentary evidence that has the potential to become the basis of proving or defending a discrimination case. Particularly in age discrimination cases, a personnel file often contains years of positive reports that turn negative at around the time an employer decides to dismiss an employee. Administrators should avoid such situations by providing honest evaluations all along, including an ongoing discussion of decline in an employee's work. Not only does the discussion in the file build a case for dismissal, but it also allows the employee—whether younger or older—the opportunity to respond to the criticism by improving his or her behavior or performance (DiGiovanni 1993a, 1993b).
- Schools and departments should develop disciplinary procedures that are progressive in nature (oral warnings should precede written warnings, which should precede suspension or dismissal), as well as a commitment to illustrating disfavored conduct for employees so they are on notice. Putting employees on notice provides them with the opportunity to comment on disciplinary actions and file an appeal. A progressive disciplinary system also affords the institution the opportunity to investigate incidents and fully document them (DiGiovanni 1993a, 1993b).
- Administrators should not discuss the specific reasons underlying negative personnel actions with employees, except under specified formal procedures. Employees typically have available grievance procedures to address any concerns about the evaluation process. Similarly, deans and chairs should not discuss with rejected job candidates the reasons why they were not hired. In the context of age discrimination, such conversations too often result in the perception by the candidate that his or her age or some other inappropriate basis was a factor (DiGiovanni 1993a, 1993b). Moreover, job descriptions for every position should reflect the actual needs of the school or department.

Affirmative action

In employment law, affirmative action programs include rules for recruitment, hiring, and promotion designed to remedy the current effects of past discrimination based on race, ethnicity, gender, or another protected group (Ruiz 1995). Designing a "safe harbor" for affirmative action employment decisions is virtually impossible, given the lack of clarity in judicial decisions addressing to what extent and within which circumstances the Fourteenth Amendment or Title VII permits affirmative action (Kaplin and Lee 1995). Poorly designed programs invite litigation by both protected groups and groups claiming "reverse discrimination" (Bernhardt 1993; Ruiz 1995). The rules for evaluating the constitutionality of affirmative action programs are somewhat different for public institutions and private institutions.

Under the Fourteenth Amendment, public institutions have an affirmative duty to eliminate the pernicious vestiges of racial and sexual discrimination in every area of their programs, including the area of employment (Ruiz 1995). Still, decisions by the U.S. Supreme Court in *Wygant v. Jackson Board of Education* (1986) and *City of Richmond v. J.A. Crowson Co.* (1989) require clear evidence of discrimination by the institution itself for race-conscious or gender-conscious hiring or promotion policies. Moreover, with the decision in *Adarand Constructors, Inc. v. Pena* (1995) (like *Crowson* not an employment case), federal race-based affirmative action programs must meet the strict scrutiny test of a demonstrated "compelling governmental interest" in having the program, policies, and procedures be as "narrowly tailored" as possible to achieve the goal of eliminating the present effects of past discrimination (L. Ware 1996). Under the holding in *Crowson,* strict scrutiny is also applied to state and local race-based affirmative action programs, including those at public colleges and universities. In *Adarand,* Justice O'Connor stated that the strict scrutiny standard in affirmative action cases is that any preference based on race or ethnicity must receive a searching examination by the court and that any review of a program must be the same whatever race or ethnicity is burdened or benefited by the program (L. Ware 1996).

The key to understanding whether a race-based affirmative action program will be constitutionally permissible under the strict scrutiny standard rests in the "compelling interest" and "narrowly tailored" standards. The logic underlying

The key to understanding whether a race-based affirmative action program will be constitutionally permissible under the strict scrutiny standard rests in the "compelling interest" and "narrowly tailored" standards.

the standards is straightforward: If the state is going to sanction treating groups differently—something expressly disfavored under the Equal Protection Clause of the Fourteenth Amendment—it must have a very good reason for doing so and must do so in a way that will damage the fewest possible people the least possible amount. The strict scrutiny standard does not mean that race-conscious remedies in hiring to eliminate discrimination will necessarily be held unconstitutional by courts, only that they must meet the compelling interest and narrowly tailored standards.

The question of whether the goal of promoting racial diversity in an academic setting—as in an affirmative action program to increase the representation of minority and women faculty—constitutes a sufficiently compelling justification to satisfy strict scrutiny remains open under the decision in *Adarand* (L. Ware 1996). The justification might work better in an academic setting, however, than in awarding construction contracts (as was at issue in *Adarand),* provided some compelling evidence exists of the impact of a more diverse faculty on the quality of campus life (as in increasing the diversity of viewpoints heard on campus) (Bell 1991; L. Ware 1996). Sufficient evidence of manifest racial imbalance in traditionally segregated job categories has met the compelling justification standard, as in the decision in *Johnson v. Transportation Agency* (1987) (Ruiz 1995). In addition, the opinion of U.S. Supreme Court Justice Powell in *Regents of the University of California v. Bakke* (1978) held that the elimination of racial discrimination in the context of admission to medical school would provide an adequate justification for the development of an affirmative action program, but that reserving certain seats in an entering class was not sufficiently narrowly tailored.

Whether a race-based hiring and promotion program will meet the narrowly tailored test depends on an examination of four factors, according to the ruling of the U.S. Supreme Court in *United States v. Paradise* (1987):

- The necessity for the relief and the efficacy of alternative remedies;
- The flexibility and duration of the program;
- The relationship of the minority hiring goals and the pool of potential minority applicants; and
- The impact of the program on nonminority employees (L. Ware 1996).

As with the compelling interest standard, how courts will interpret the narrowly tailored test in the academic context is an open question.

At private institutions, voluntary efforts to address a manifest racial imbalance in the labor market in a traditionally segregated field are permissible under the decision in *Weber v. Kaiser Aluminum Co.* (1979), provided they do not unnecessarily trammel the rights of white employees and no explicit quotas are established (Leap 1995). Proving that a manifest imbalance exists through statistical or other evidence is sometimes difficult, however. In the academic context, voluntary affirmative action programs intended to create a more favorable racial balance or diversity on a faculty or in the administrative ranks would likely be upheld, provided the programs:

- Were temporary;
- Did not completely prevent the advancement of white and male candidates;
- Did not set aside a specific number of positions for minorities;
- Did not force the termination of white or male candidates to make room for nonminority candidates; and
- Were flexible in approach and considered each case individually (Leap 1995).

Finally, the lawfulness of gender-based affirmative action programs instituted by public employers is generally measured under an "intermediate" level of scrutiny (as opposed to strict scrutiny in race-based cases). Courts uphold the legality of a plan if the relevant gender classifications are substantially related to an important governmental objective, as stated by the U.S. Supreme Court in *Mississippi University for Women v. Hogan* (1982) (Ruiz 1995). Whether a plan is substantially related to an important governmental objective is measured by the actual advantage given to women (even in areas where women are not disadvantaged) and the degree of burden that the program places upon men (Ruiz 1995). The important governmental objective test is less stringent than the compelling governmental justification test applied to race-based programs. For instance, the desire to remedy societal discrimination encountered by women—provided that any claim of discrimination is accompanied by adequate evidence—may be a sufficiently important objective (Ruiz 1995). Providing "role models" for students would likely not support a gender-based affirmative action program in the academic setting, however (Ruiz 1995).

Reappointment, tenure, and promotion

Like decisions about hiring, decisions about conferring tenure come with high stakes. A negative decision can derail the academic career of a faculty member, just as an ill-advised decision to grant tenure can slow or disrupt a school or department for years (Leap 1995). In addition, tenure litigation exacts a substantial financial, social, and psychological cost for the individuals and institutions involved (Leap 1995). Courts have typically granted institutions broad freedom from judicial scrutiny in such decisions, deferring to the asserted superior experience and expertise of administrators and faculty committees in the area (Paretsky 1993; Swedlow 1994). Nevertheless, courts will reverse negative tenure decisions when sufficient evidence exists of discrimination in making the determination or when decisions are arbitrary or made in bad faith (Leas 1991; Paretsky 1993).

Even though the basic framework for achieving tenure is common across most schools, the requirements to actually receive tenure may differ greatly, not only from university to university but also between and among schools and departments at the same university (Swedlow 1994). Nevertheless, tenure has three general coordinate elements across institutions:

- It enables faculty members to teach and study free of restraints and pressures that would otherwise inhibit independent thought and action.
- Tenure marks a type of communal acceptance into the professional guild by faculty peers.
- Tenure provides the job security that encourages loyalty and rewards accomplishment (McHugh 1973).

Tenure is generally an up-or-out proposition. Under AAUP guidelines, which many institutions have incorporated into their own rules, all regular faculty have tenure or the expectation is they are capable of achieving it. The AAUP mandates a probationary period not to exceed seven years, after which faculty receive tenure or are not offered reemployment for the next academic year (Leap 1995; McKee 1980). During the probationary period, faculty typically receive a series of annual (or sometimes multiyear) appointments. Probationary faculty can be terminated at the end of any of those appointments.

The procedure to receive tenure is commonly outlined in an institution's written rules and regulations and characteristically entails a pyramid of reviewing committees where recommendations made at one level can later be reversed at a higher level. A typical structure originates with a committee in the department or school. Applications next move through a campuswide tenure committee to the provost and president, who then present a recommendation to the governing board for final approval (McHugh 1973). The governing board is usually the entity in which the authority to grant tenure is vested. Courts are mixed on the question of whether the board can delegate this authority (Hendrickson 1990; Paretsky 1993). Most institutions have an internal appeals process for negative decisions (Leap 1995; J. Mullaney and Timberlake 1994).

A confluence of several factors usually shapes the decision to grant or deny tenure, including not only a particular candidate's scholarly credentials but also general budgetary, economic, staffing, and related nonacademic concerns (McHugh 1973). Generally, the academic qualifications of individual applicants focus on subjective and objective measures of quality in four key areas: research and scholarship; classroom teaching; institutional, professional, and community service; and collegial relations with other faculty (Paretsky 1993). Evidence of these qualifications comes from the candidate himself or herself, often through a portfolio that includes examples of publications, evaluations, and commendations, as well as from reviews prepared by faculty in the same discipline at other institutions (J. Mullaney and Timberlake 1994).

The key to understanding the decision is that criteria cannot be quantified and defined precisely, lest institutions risk abandoning the flexibility that allows for decisions in the best interests of their academic missions (Leap 1995). Although applicants and committees attempt to measure these constructs objectively and subjectively, it is difficult to make a concrete calculation of the quality (or even the quantity) of activities like research, teaching, service, and collegiality.

Accordingly, courts have been exceedingly reluctant to upset administrative evaluations of faculty merit, citing their general lack of expertise regarding the criteria for attaining tenure, the institutional implications of the decision, and the sanctity of academic freedom at institutions of higher education (Leap 1995). Courts have usually upheld any reason for denying tenure that relates in some way to the quality, efficiency, or philosophy of the institution (Paretsky 1993). In research, denials of tenure have been upheld by courts for insufficient or unexceptional output, failure to obtain a terminal degree, and failure to conform with a department's changing expectations for research. In teaching, courts have upheld negative decisions for having a teaching philosophy incompatible with the institutions's pedagogical aims and poor teaching evaluations by students, but they generally do not accept rejections of tenure in retaliation for constitutionally protected speech (Hendrickson 1990). Institutional needs are also important, and courts have allowed negative decisions to stand when a candidate's expertise was outside the institution's mission, when limited institutional resources did not allow for the expansion of tenured faculty, and when the number of faculty in a department argued against adding another tenured member. Finally, decisions based on collegiality are usually upheld when noncollegial behavior is not used as a pretext for ideological disagreements, denial of academic freedom, or discrimination (J. Mullaney and Timberlake 1994; Zirkel 1985).

Therefore, as a basic rule, if the administration has any legitimate reason for denying tenure, the reason will likely suffice, even if other criteria support granting tenure and even if the faculty member is a member of a protected group under the discrimination laws (Leap 1995; Paretsky 1993). In other words, reasons for denying tenure are usually legitimate provided they are not based on some constitutionally impermissible ground (racial discrimination, for example) or in retaliation for asserting rights guaranteed under the law (First Amendment rights, for example). Courts have held that institutions need not provide reasons for denying tenure, except when a protected class or fundamental right is involved (Paretsky 1993). Moreover, institutions do not need to apply the same factors to different candidates for tenure, and various departments within an institution can have different standards for granting tenure (Paretsky 1993). Finally, institutions can also use minority status to break ties between or among individuals with equal qualifications (Leap 1995).

When institutions have violated their own policies on tenure or when a decision is found to be unreasonable, arbitrary, or capricious, courts will usually order a new tenure review to be conducted, purged of the error. In addition, preliminary relief may be extended to plaintiffs—an injunction against termination before a grievance hearing is resolved, for instance—as well as economic remedies, including compensatory damages (lost wages, for instance), punitive damages, and attorneys' fees (Leap 1995). In some extreme cases, the court may feel compelled to actually award tenure (Hendrickson 1990).

Typically, plaintiffs have challenged negative decisions under a discrimination theory or a contract theory. Discrimination lawsuits are generally based on the argument of disparate treatment, with the plaintiff alleging that the institution treated him or her less favorably than others on the basis of some immutable characteristic, including the areas protected by Title VII (race, ethnicity, sex, religion), the ADA (disability), and the ADEA (age) (Swedlow 1994). A situation involving disparate impact is also possible if an institutionwide or systemwide policy that seems neutral has the effect of discriminating against an entire class of individuals (Leap 1995).

The framework applied by courts to decide cases of disparate treatment in disputes about tenure is the same as in other employment actions: The plaintiff must make a reasonable suggestion that discrimination occurred in the decision, which the institution must then rebut by articulating a legitimate nondiscriminatory reason for the rejection of tenure, and then the plaintiff must prove the reason proffered by the institution was merely a pretext (Swedlow 1994). In short, discrimination actions will probably not be successful if the institution:

- Has followed its own specified procedures;
- Has based its decisions on neutrally applied criteria related to research, teaching, service, and collegiality;
- Did not discriminate with respect to categories of individuals who are protected under Title VII, the ADA, and the ADEA; and
- Did not structure the tenure review committee in a way that favors one group over another (Hendrickson 1990).

In discrimination cases, the EEOC is allowed access to materials reviewed in the tenure decision, records of the tenure committee's deliberations, and materials used to evaluate the tenure decisions of others within a relevant period of time (Hendrickson 1990; Lee 1990; Shaw 1991). Often, information in tenure review files—departmental evaluations, minutes of the tenure committee's meetings, letters from outside reviewers, and so on—is intended to be kept confidential (Copeland and Murry 1996; Sarchet 1995), but the success or failure of a challenge to a tenure decision often depends upon just such information's being made available as evidence for the rejected candidate. The decision of the U.S. Supreme Court in *University of Pennsylvania v. EEOC* (1990) upheld the right of the Equal Employment Opportunity Commission to subpoena files in investigating discrimination in cases involving tenure. Part of the significance of the case is that access to peer review materials is just the kind of information that is critical to plaintiffs as evidence in making a case against a negative tenure evaluation (Lee 1990; Yeung 1995). The case involved competing interests: the institution's concern for preserving the confidentiality of peer review and the need for relevant evidence when disappointed faculty suspect that a negative tenure decision is the result of illegal bias (Lee 1990). The Supreme Court rejected the institution's argument that institutional academic freedom justified retaining confidentiality at all costs and held that any injury to academic freedom was speculative (Bednash 1991; Sarchet 1995). Although some evaluators might be less candid as the possibility of disclosure increases, most reviewers would simply ground their evaluations in specific illustrations to deflect potential claims of bias or unfairness (Burke and Cavaliere 1991). The Court found neither a qualified privilege preventing the disclosure of peer review materials nor a privilege grounded in academic freedom protecting confidentiality (Grexa 1992; R. Robinson, Franklin, and Allen 1990; Shaw 1991).

Institutions must now provide the EEOC with access to all peer evaluation materials that the commission deems relevant to investigating complaints of discrimination. The *University of Pennsylvania* decision, however, did not address whether an institution could avoid problems of confidentiality by omitting names and other identifying features from documents produced (Lee 1990). Moreover, state laws permitting access to documents and records of meetings at public institutions may also open promotion and tenure records to those interested in obtaining them. As a result of the *University of Pennsylvania* decision, external reviewers should be made aware of the possibility that their comments made during tenure reviews could become public (Leap 1995; Lee 1990).

In contract-based actions involving rejections of tenure, plaintiffs may argue that their employment contracts imply a right to a tenure review procedure consistent with stated institutional policy and the concepts of fundamental fairness. Faculty handbooks listing standards and procedures applied in tenure determinations could be a cited source of institutional policy (J. Mullaney and Timberlake 1994). Decisions about tenure are likely to be upheld when institutions perform their obligations under the employment contract. These obligations are usually straightforward, and committees must follow stated institutional procedures and agreed-upon practices in deliberations. They must also base decisions on substantive reasons supported by evidence, in accord with stated tenure criteria, and on factors consistent with institutional missions (J. Mullaney and Timberlake 1994). Finally, when simple procedural shortcomings in a tenure review decision do not have a prejudicial effect, courts will typically ignore the technical violations and uphold the decision (Hendrickson 1990; Paretsky 1993).

Attempts to extend the requirements of constitutional due process to the tenure review process have generally been futile, as nontenured employees have no legitimate expectation of tenure (Hendrickson 1990; Olswang and Fantel 1980). Constitutional due process protection arises only after tenure has actually been afforded to faculty at public institutions (Bednash 1991; Paretsky 1993). Probationary faculty who are denied tenure at public institutions do not have a property interest in continued employment and thus no real due process rights. Institutional policies, state personnel laws, or contract provisions, however, often require timely notification and permit faculty a formal hearing if their contracts are not going to be renewed (Leap 1995). Due process protection afforded to all faculty at private institutions is a matter of stated institutional policies, and academic custom and practice—particularly when the AAUP's guidelines for tenure have been adopted by the institution—as well as whatever protections state contract law affords.

Five types of situations involving discrimination in tenure decisions could precipitate lawsuits after a negative decision:

1. A lack of institutional support and resources made it difficult for a faculty member to achieve an acceptable level of performance. In these cases, the faculty member claims that inadequate resources, low funding, or heavy teaching and service loads made it difficult or impossible to fulfill expectations for tenure, particularly in the area of research.

In contract-based actions involving rejections of tenure, plaintiffs may argue that their employment contracts imply a right to a tenure review procedure consistent with stated institutional policy and the concepts of fundamental fairness.

2. The institution failed to adhere to its own standards for promotion and tenure. The allegation here is that the criteria explained to the faculty member during the probationary period by his or her dean or chair—and under which he or she labored for several years—were not the ones applied by the tenure committee and administrators involved in determining whether tenure would be granted.
3. Political rather than academic reasons led to the unfavorable decision about promotion or tenure. In these types of cases, the faculty member accuses the administration of favoring certain faculty over others and applying different performance standards to similarly situated faculty when it makes personnel decisions, causing politics to be the basis of the decision instead of merit.
4. The institution failed to consistently apply standards for promotion and tenure. Here, the faculty member contends that a denial of reappointment, tenure, or promotion was unfair because similarly situated faculty with inferior credentials received more favorable treatment. Such claims are usually supported by comparisons between the academic credentials of the rejected faculty member with recently tenured faculty. Cases also sometimes revolve around allegations that provosts or presidents making the final decision on a tenure application are not qualified to evaluate the scholarship of faculty working in particular disciplines and so are inconsistent in their treatment of them.
5. Review committees and others involved in the decision harbored racist, sexist, or other prejudices. In these cases, the faculty member accuses the administration of applying irrelevant factors, such as race or sex, to academic decisions. Plaintiffs may bolster their cases by blaming administrators for creating a hostile working environment in which racist or sexist attitudes were condoned (Leap 1995).

These situations can often be avoided with improved practice in a school or department. Deans and chairs might consider improved processes for recruiting and selecting faculty, as well as augmented orientation and career development for faculty, including mentoring programs. A school's or department's criteria and standards for promotion and tenure can also be made clearer when needed. Improved working conditions—including protections against forms of harassment, allocations of appropriate time and resources to meet the criteria for tenure, and enhanced collegiality and working relationships with colleagues—would all reduce the potential for litigation. The same can be said of better recognition and understanding of interruptions to a career and family responsibilities. And deans and chairs would be wise to offer more complete and better-communicated faculty performance evaluations (Leap 1995).

As in all employment-related issues, deans and chairs should maintain careful and complete records. Notes from annual evaluations of faculty and meetings with faculty during which tenure or expectations for tenure are discussed should be recorded in writing and shared with each faculty member evaluated. Should litigation ensue, a dean's or chair's personal notes not shared with the candidate could become evidence of the school's or department's unwillingness to communicate accurate evaluation criteria (Drapeau 1995). The bottom line is that academic administrators should follow the university's procedures for granting tenure carefully and act in good faith (Drapeau 1995; Gillepsie 1985). Courts are inclined to defer to administrative judgment in cases involving tenure, absent evidence that the decision was arbitrary, discriminatory, or made in bad faith. Finally, academic administrators may be named as defendants in lawsuits along with the institution. They are typically fully indemnified by the institution for any damages that the plaintiff recovers, provided they follow these simple rules (Drapeau 1995).

Personnel issues at religious institutions
Institutions having some connection with religion—in control, administration, or support—fall into three main categories:

- Institutions founded as church related (Harvard or Oberlin, for instance) that have evolved into essentially secular institutions, indistinguishable in curriculum and institutional character from secular institutions generally;
- Previously church-related schools founded by ethnic groups (Calvin College by the Dutch Reformed Church or Gustavus Adolphus College by Swedish Lutherans, for instance) that now are distinguished by environmental or cultural characteristics rather than ideological or doctrinal ones; and
- Institutions that have retained a strong spiritual identity (Catholic University or Brigham Young University, for in-

stance) and attract students and faculty willing to conform to particular religious and cultural constraints (Julius 1991).

It is the third group of universities and colleges that are generally involved in personnel issues connected with religion.

These institutions are generally different from sectarian institutions in several ways, and the differences have an often profound impact on personnel matters. Collegiality is often more pronounced at religiously affiliated institutions. Because religious institutions are often grounded in different purposes from secular institutions, individuals employed at denominational colleges often view their work as more of a calling than an occupation (Duchin 1991). And because resources are often limited and pay is typically low at these schools, many services are commonly donated or volunteered (Julius 1991). The environment in religiously affiliated institutions often promotes generosity in performance evaluations, in recognition of the sacrifices attendant to working at a church-related school and in furtherance of the values of community and collegiality (Duchin 1991).

As a result of their distinctive character, religiously affiliated institutions have some degree of exemption from requirements for nondiscrimination in hiring and employment (Araujo 1996; Leap 1995). To protect the religious character of church-related schools, courts have allowed for preferential hiring based on religion in certain circumstances, under the "bona fide occupational qualification" doctrine. For example, church-related institutions are allowed to discriminate somewhat in hiring—limiting their hiring to ordained ministers to teach seminary students or members of a religious order to teach philosophy at an institution affiliated with that order, for example—even if these criteria inherently exclude other groups, particularly women (Araujo 1996).

The principle of nondiscrimination articulated in Title VII and elsewhere has three types of exceptions (Araujo 1996). Although the exceptions do not give institutions the explicit right to discriminate, they preclude the imposition of sanctions or injunctions against the institution in certain types of situations:

- When personal adherence to the principles of a certain religion is needed to continue the missions and activities of the institution, as, for example, hiring an ordained minister with certain religious beliefs as campus chaplain. Religiously affiliated schools can thus refuse to hire or can discharge someone whose personal conduct—say an out-of-wedlock birth or support of abortion rights—is counter to the institution's religious tenets. The exception would extend even to the dismissal of a tenured faculty member.

- When the religion or religious views of a candidate or employee are integral to what is reasonably necessary to ensure the successful operation of the institution—for example, the interest at some religiously affiliated institutions in maintaining a sizable core of faculty belonging to the sponsoring religion to maintain the character of the institution.
- When hiring practices based on religious affiliation are geared toward perpetuating a curriculum that is directed toward propagation of a particular religion (Laycock 1993).

Nevertheless, the U.S. Supreme Court has drawn the line at certain types of discrimination in the context of religion. In *Bob Jones University v. United States* (1983), a case involving institutional rules against interracial dating, the court held that the interest in racial equality in education is such a compelling interest that it overrides the free exercise of religious rights. The logic underlying the ruling is that religious claims about race are likely insincere and that even sincere beliefs in racial discrimination are less central to most religious traditions than theology or sexual morality (Laycock 1993).

Practical Concerns in Hiring and Promotion
Employment interviews
Several state and federal laws govern the areas about which employers can question prospective employees during interviews (Carkeek et al. 1988; Ford 1993; Marchese and Lawrence 1988; Pullum 1991). Such questions—whether direct or indirect—can be used to discriminate on the basis of a category protected under Title VII and other antidiscrimination legislation. In general, questions related to job requirements and the applicant's ability to meet them are permitted. Questions that seek to identity information that might be used to discriminate are disfavored.

- Employers cannot ask about marital status, pregnancy, future plans to raise children, and the number and ages of children (Pullum 1991). For example, an employer can ask an applicant whether he or she has commitments that may impede attending meetings or job responsibilities but cannot ask about specific arrangements for child care (Ford 1993). Other questions intended to restrict employment on the basis of gender are permissible only in the very rare cases when gender is a bona fide occupational qualification (BFOQ). For example, questions related to the height or weight of an applicant—often used as a surrogate for gender—must be avoided unless height and weight are necessary requirements for the position, as might be the case in hiring certain security personnel (but is likely rare elsewhere in higher education) (Ford 1993). Similarly, unless age is a BFOQ, employers are advised not to ask the age of the applicant (Ford 1993). Finally, questions about the origins of an applicant's name, or requests for his or her photograph are discouraged, given their potential to be used to identify race, ethnicity, or gender (Ford 1993).

• The ADA prohibits questions directed at the nature and severity of any physical or mental disabilities. It also protects against employers' imposing job requirements that disadvantage those with disabilities, unless an institutional necessity exists for the requirement and accommodating the disabled person would impose an undue hardship on the institution. Discrimination against those who smoke is not necessarily prohibited under the ADA, however. Although legislation in some states may allow deference to nonsmokers, laws in other states and certain municipalities prohibit disadvantaging smokers in making employment decisions (Ford 1993). Another developing area of law is drug and alcohol screening for applicants. Academic administrators are advised to consult counsel to determine the standing in their jurisdiction of including consideration of voluntary behavior generally associated with poor health in the decision to hire someone.

Finally, no federal law prohibits discrimination on the basis of physical appearance. Employers may establish reasonable standards of dress and grooming, provided they are uniformly applied and do not have a disproportionate impact on members of classes protected under the antidiscrimination laws (Ford 1993).

• Although federal law has not recognized sexual orientation as a protected class under the antidiscrimination laws, refusal to hire a qualified candidate on the basis of sexual orientation alone may violate certain federal or state constitutional rights, state or local laws, or institutional policies (Ford 1993). Moreover, academic administrators should be aware of institutional policies extending benefits to domestic partners (Fried 1994; Laarman 1993).

- Employers may not discriminate on the basis of national origin. Specific inquiry is prohibited into information that would indicate national origin, such as foreign addresses, or the origin or birthplace of an applicant. Similarly, employers may not ask what country an applicant is a citizen of or whether the applicant or any relative is a U.S. citizen (Ford 1993). Questions related to the ability to submit proof of citizenship after hiring are permitted, however (Ford 1993). Employers may ask whether an applicant is a citizen of the United States, has the right to remain permanently in this country, or is prevented from lawfully becoming employed because of visa or immigration status. In addition, employers may inquire about the applicant's fluency in English, but questions related to national origin or native language are forbidden (Ford 1993).

- The same is true of educational status and work experience. Employers may ask questions related to educational attainment and schools attended, but they may not frame these inquiries in terms of an applicant's nationality, racial association, or religious affiliation of a school attended, nor can they ask how the applicant gained his or her ability in English. Employers may ask about the names and addresses of previous employers, dates of employment, reasons for leaving, and salary history (Ford 1993).

- Employers may not inquire into an applicant's religious preference, denominational affiliation, or church attended unless they are BFOQs. It is permissible to inquire about organizations of which the applicant is a member, provided the name or character of the organization does not reveal the race, religion, or ancestry of the job candidate (Ford 1993). Similarly, employers may advise applicants of work requirements to avoid possible conflicts with religious or other convictions (Ford 1993).

- Courts also do not allow questions about arrest records without proof of institutional necessity. Questions about actual convictions are permissible, although under EEOC guidelines, conviction may not be an absolute bar to employment (Ford 1993). Those making hiring decisions should consider mitigating factors such as the frequency and severity of the violations, age of the applicant at the time of the illegal act, time elapsed since the conviction, and so on in determining the weight that a conviction should have in the decision to hire someone. In addition, employers may not ask what type of military discharge a veteran received (Ford 1993).

- Federal law limits the circumstances under which employers may test employees using polygraph examinations, including exceptions for certain defense and intelligence contractors (Ford 1993). Similarly, inquiry into financial information—including overall assets, home or automobile ownership, or past wage garnishments—is prohibited, as is the use of credit reports, unless it is institutionally necessary to do so (Ford 1993).

Those conducting interviews and making hiring decisions must exercise care. The emerging tort of negligent hiring holds employers liable for the failure to discover key information about an employee that reasonably might have prevented harm and liability to others from that employee's actions. In addition, vicarious liability—where the employer is held responsible for certain acts of employees—can result from placing unfit employees into positions (Ford 1993).

Aside from issues related to what questions may and may not be asked during an interview, affirmative action is typically an issue in searches at universities and colleges. Federal law requires search committees to make a "good faith effort" to develop a talent pool reflecting the available women and minorities in the labor force (Marchese and Lawrence 1988). How the committee ensures that it has met the standard is an open question. It is suggested that the effort should equal or exceed that expended on getting other valued people into the institution, such as recruiting the best students (Marchese and Lawrence 1988). The affirmative action office at an institution may also have analyzed imbalances in staffing on the campus and could provide the academic administrator with general guidance (Carkeek et al. 1988). In the end, an affirmative action–based legal challenge will be decided on whether the institution has made a full good faith effort overall in the area of affirmative action and whether the effort has succeeded in terms of the hiring and promotion of women and people of color on campus (Marchese and Lawrence 1988).

Nevertheless, keeping applications of minority or women candidates under consideration when they have no real potential to be appointed to the position or successful in it is typically a poor decision. A better practice is to stop the search process and renew recruiting efforts for the position (Marchese and Lawrence 1988). Further, deans and chairs should refrain from indicating that they are interested *only* in hiring a woman or minority candidate to improve the unit's diversity (Ford 1993). To ensure fairness for all candidates, especially women or minority candidates, those involved in hiring should require the same standards of all applicants and ask the same general questions of each (Ford 1993).

Moreover, seemingly benign personal questions—those related to marital status, plans to raise children, child care, a spouse's employment, willingness to travel or work long hours—can assume a gender-based significance, particularly for women. Similarly, certain information about a place—that a small college town is a good place to raise children or a difficult place for a single person or minority, for instance—is value laden. The same is true of other gender-based prejudices—that men are ill-suited for secretarial positions or that women are too emotional to become leaders, for example (Ford 1993).

Finally, when an applicant believes discrimination has occurred, he or she can file a complaint with the EEOC or applicable state agency, bring a lawsuit against the prospective employer, or file a class action with other similarly aggrieved plaintiffs (Pullum 1991). Still, the plaintiff must specifically establish in concrete terms how the discrimination occurred during the selection process (Pullum 1991). If the plaintiff is successful, courts will award remedies—sometimes substantial remedies—ranging from money damages to orders enjoining future wrongdoing (Pullum 1991).

To avoid these problems, academic administrators involved in searches should arrange briefings, as appropriate, with legal, personnel, and affirmative action staff so that they understand relevant federal, state, and local statutes and guidelines, and applicable institutional regulations and policy statements (Marchese and Lawrence 1988). The keys to avoiding legal difficulties in a search include:

- Learning what a search committee can and cannot do;
- Remaining open, consistent, and fair throughout the process; and

To avoid these problems, academic administrators involved in searches should arrange briefings, as appropriate, with legal, personnel, and affirmative action staff.

- Keeping good records of procedures determined for the search and decisions made (Marchese and Lawrence 1988).*

Individual privacy rights

The Fourth Amendment enters into higher education in two principle ways. Constitutional protections against warrantless and unreasonable searches and seizures are sometimes an issue in residence halls at public institutions where residence life and student affairs staff are state actors. Deans and chairs are more likely to be involved in the other usual Fourth Amendment issue: drug testing. The two issues are likely the subject of institutionwide policies. Given their complexity, academic administrators should consult university counsel for guidance when the issues arise.

At public institutions, testing is typically a Fourth Amendment issue because it is, in essence, a search and seizure. The standard for determining whether a drug testing policy is constitutionally valid is whether any intrusion caused by the actual testing outweighs a legitimate governmental interest in preventing the behavior that the testing is intended to prevent (Kaplin and Lee 1995). Drug testing involves a high level of intrusiveness. Courts have held urinalysis to be a significant intrusion into a fundamentally private domain. Other issues are related to the reliability of tests (American Association of University 1992). Therefore, a legitimate interest must rise to the level of protecting public safety or sensitive information (James, Gomez, and Bulgar 1995). The U.S. Supreme Court allowed drug testing policies at the U.S. Customs Service for employees carrying firearms or confiscating drugs in *National Treasury Employees Union v. Von Raabe* (1989). The Court also allowed rules mandated by the Federal Railroad Administration requiring blood and urine testing for drugs and alcohol after certain violations of safety rules in *Skinner v. Railway Labor Executives Association* (1989). In both cases, the Court found it persuasive that the employees were part of a pervasively regulated industry (Kaplin and Lee 1995).

At public postsecondary institutions, the question is whether the testing program—whether mandatory testing of all employees or random testing based on individual suspi-

---

*Marchese and Lawrence's monograph offers an excellent review of best practices in the search process.

cion—is justified by the dangers of impaired professional fitness as a result of substance abuse (American Association of University 1992). It seems difficult to argue that faculty and administrators in higher education are engaged in a profession where the use of controlled substances poses a safety hazard to colleagues, constituents, or to society in general (Kaplin and Lee 1995). The AAUP (1992) argues that no valid purpose for universal or random drug testing programs exists in the academic community, favoring instead the observation of employees to identify deficient performance related to the use of drugs rather than the excessive intrusion that results from the testing.

At private institutions, where the U.S. Constitution is inapplicable, certain state constitutions (including California and Illinois) provide a right to privacy under which employees could challenge a testing policy. In addition, some cities, including San Francisco, have adopted ordinances related to testing (Stadler 1989). (The right to privacy read into the Constitution by the U.S. Supreme Court in *Griswold v. Connecticut* [1965] and other cases is limited to issues related to procreation.) Certain common law causes of action—invasion of privacy, negligence, defamation, wrongful discharge—may also offer potential plaintiffs relief, even if testing programs are within federal and other provisions (Stadler 1989). Finally, the ADA protects individuals with certain alcohol- and drug-related addictions from discrimination on the basis of that addiction.

Certain types of other testing—genetic testing, HIV and AIDS testing, polygraph testing, psychological or personality testing, obtaining credit information—typically are expressly prohibited by federal or state statutes for both private and public employers (James, Gomez, and Bulgar 1995).

Immigration

Although institutions typically have routines for processing the increasing number of work permits and visas received each year for international faculty and staff—often for foreign-trained faculty and instructors in engineering and the sciences—each document "requires intricate detail, elaborate paperwork, and administrative nudging to negotiate the arcane process. The laws are complex, the regulations contradictory and unclear, and the rules of the game . . . shifting and idiosyncratic" (Olivas 1992, p. 573). Despite the fact that deans and chairs routinely refer immigration questions to a designated office on campus, it is important for academic administrators to appreciate the general parameters of federal immigration laws.

Congress has broad authority to draw distinctions on the basis of nationality in the context of immigration (Kaplin and Lee 1995). The foundation of U.S. immigration law is the Immigration and Naturalization Act of 1952, which established per-year and per-country ceilings on immigration. Under the act, preferences are given to immigrants with family connections or employment arranged in the United States (D. Ware, Somers, and Speake 1993). Three profound changes in immigration law occurred during the 1980s. First, the Refugee Act of 1989 established a uniform policy for people fleeing religious, political, or other persecution (D. Ware, Somers, and Speake 1993). Second, the Immigration Reform and Control Act of 1986 provided processes to legalize many undocumented workers residing in the United States and penalize employers for hiring undocumented workers (Simon 1992). Third, the Immigration Marriage Fraud Act created a two-year conditional residency period to test the viability of a marriage for aliens seeking to immigrate based on marriage to a U.S. citizen.

The Immigration Act of 1990 overhauled U.S. immigration law by:

- Expanding preferences for granting immigration and increasing emphasis on immigration by skilled laborers;
- Promoting diversity in immigration by establishing a lottery for countries sending few immigrants to the United States; and
- Permitting persons creating substantial sources of employment in the United States the right to obtain lawful personal residence (D. Ware, Somers, and Speake 1993).

The act also ended prohibitions on the immigration of gays and lesbians, people with mental disorders, "subversives," and communists (Simon 1992).

An important distinction in immigration law is the one between nonimmigrants, who come to the United States for a specific purpose and limited amount of time, and immigrants, who legally come to the United States to live and work permanently (D. Ware, Somers, and Speake 1993). The Immigration and Naturalization Service (INS) grants nonimmigrant status to a person entering the country. Types of nonimmigrant status can be changed by petition to the INS. Aliens who have entered the country illegally, exceeded their designated period of admission, or deviated from their particular category of nonimmigrant status are termed "undocumented" under the immigration laws. The INS also enforces its rules against employers who hire undocumented workers.

The visa that provides someone permission to enter the United States is obtained through the Department of State at a U.S. consulate abroad. The H-1B nonimmigrant visa is the primary means used to arrange for the employment of international faculty and staff, despite its somewhat protracted and cumbersome procedures (D. Ware, Somers, and Speake 1993). The visa category is intended for aliens coming temporarily to the country to perform services in a specialty occupation for which a bachelor's degree or its equivalent is needed. Employers must attest to the Department of Labor that the worker will be paid market wages, work within prevailing conditions, and is not replacing workers engaged in a strike or lockout. The employer must certify to the INS that the prospective position is a specialty occupation, that the alien has the appropriate qualifications, and that the employer will pay the reasonable costs of return transportation should the alien be fired during the period of authorized H-1B status (D. Ware, Somers, and Speake 1993).

Faculty and staff who petition for lawful permanent resident status can be employed permanently and can change positions at will. To hire an alien permanently, an employer must certify that no U.S. worker is available to fill the position.

All new hires, foreign and domestic, must document that they are eligible to work in the United States by completing Form I-4. Preemployment inquiries are limited, however, especially when they are made only to those who appear to be foreign born. Accordingly, academic administrators should carefully follow institutional policies on employing international staff and scholars and make sure they understand the applicable rules before signing I-4s.

Certain tax issues are involved in employing foreign nationals that turn on both visa status and exemptions available through one of several international tax treaties (D. Ware, Somers, and Speake 1993). Moreover, difficulties sometimes arise when international faculty and staff are in the United States on a visitor or student visa and they perform some task for a school or department for which the institution wishes to compensate them. As with other procedural issues in immigration, the key for deans or chairs is to recognize that the procedures involved with obtaining the necessary status for international faculty and staff are complex and that people with the expertise to navigate the various procedures involved are usually available on campus.

Conduct and Misconduct on the Job: Navigating The Employment Relationship
Academic freedom

"Academic freedom is a well-established tradition in American higher education, yet its metes and bounds are far from precise" (Newman 1995, p. 289). Individuals, institutions, and courts often ascribe different meanings to the concept. In theory, academic freedom applies to individual faculty members and students as well as to institutions, but the courts have not expressly recognized the differences between academic freedom as applied to individual faculty and individual institutions and the concept of academic freedom for students is much less developed than that for faculty and institutions (Doughtrey 1991). The bases of academic freedom are in the German concepts of *lehrfreiheit* (teaching freedom), *lernfreiheit* (learning freedom), and *freiheit der wessenschaft* (academic self-government) (Doughtrey 1991; Kaplin and Lee 1995; Olswang and Fantel 1980). The societal rationale for academic freedom is preserving and encouraging the robust exchange of ideas within a community of scholars (Doughtrey 1991; Smolla 1990).

Under the 1940 AAUP Statement of Principles, academic freedom for faculty is the ability to pursue teaching and research goals—no matter how controversial—and to enjoy the same right to free expression as others in society without fear of negative employment consequences (Doughtrey 1991; Newman 1995; Olivas 1993; Olswang 1988; Van Alstyne 1993). Academic freedom protects not only faculty from their own institutions, governing boards, government agencies, and legislatures, but also institutions from government interference (Newman 1995). Moreover, faculty appointment is immaterial to academic freedom. Under the 1940 AAUP statement, probationary faculty have the same right to academic freedom as do tenured faculty (Doughtrey 1991; Kaplin and Lee 1995).

Definitions of academic freedom are both professional—the one articulated by the AAUP—and legal—the one centered in the First and Fourteenth Amendments (Metzger 1993). The professional side of academic freedom is often a question of contract law. It either is incorporated into faculty contracts directly, through stated institutional policy, or is implied through an institution's academic custom and usage (Lovely 1991). At private institutions, contract law is essentially the limit of the protection of academic freedom. Similarly, academic freedom is based on contract in religious settings as a result of concerns about the Establishment Clause and the Free Exercise Clause. Religious institutions are expressly excluded from the AAUP's 1940 Statement, based on the argument that the production of knowledge or its dissemination in print and in classrooms often refers to doctrinal authority (Kaplin and Lee 1995).

At public universities and colleges, academic freedom is linked with constitutional principles. In *Sweezy v. New Hampshire* (1957), the U.S. Supreme Court indicated that academic freedom is a particularly cherished First Amendment right (Hiers 1995; Lovely 1991). Nevertheless, courts have not specifically held that a distinct right to academic freedom exists (Olswang and Fantel 1980). As in *Sweezy,* statements emphasizing the importance of free inquiry to a free society are often in dicta. (Dicta are writings in a judicial opinion that are not necessarily a basis of the decision and thus are not binding as legal precedent.) The famous and expansive statement by Justice Frankfurter in *Sweezy* in support of academic freedom as necessary to a "free society" is in a concurring opinion (an opinion agreeing with the decision of the majority, but for different reasons). Frankfurter portrayed academic freedom at the university as four essential freedoms: "to determine for itself on academic grounds who may teach, what may be taught, how it shall be taught, and who may be admitted to study" (Doughtrey 1991). Thus, academic freedom is recognized by the courts but does not have the status of a concrete constitutional principle. Finally, at public institutions, academic freedom may also be the subject of state statutes or administrative regulations (Kaplin and Lee 1995).

Early academic freedom cases typically involved external intrusions (Hiers 1995; Lovely 1991). The 1915 AAUP Declaration of Principles was concerned with governing boards and legislatures, specifically within the contexts of judicial deference for trustees' authority and the potential for intolerance of faculty members' exploration that challenged the status quo (Olswang 1988). The Declaration articulated several rights and privileges for faculty, including reappointment through faculty committee, the right to tenure with a probationary period not to exceed seven years, notice of grounds for dismissal, and a hearing before dismissal (Kaplin and Lee 1995). Later academic freedom cases generally involved institutional intrusions against individuals. In the 1940s and 1950s, several court decisions applied First Amendment principles to determine that institutions could not terminate faculty for membership in political organizations, could not require disclaimer oaths, and could not engage in "fishing expeditions" to seek information related to professional associations, competence, or integrity (Lovely 1991).

Different areas of faculty life are protected differently, and research is the most protected area. Although courts have usually been willing to protect the integrity of research, scholars have no absolute privilege when there is an appropriate need to release research data. Protection of academic freedom for activities in the classroom is weakest, given the institution's interest in maintaining the integrity of instructional activities. Still, institutions have authority over instructional activities (but not absolute authority). Indeed, the U.S. Supreme Court has never spoken categorically on teaching freedom (Metzger 1993).

Academic freedom is also protected for faculty in their nonteaching and nonresearch activities, typically those involving expression.

Academic freedom is also protected for faculty in their nonteaching and nonresearch activities, typically those involving expression. In addition, academics have a limited right to outside employment, provided it does not interfere with the substantial interests of the institution (Kaplin and Lee 1995). Discussions of matters of public concern are protected, provided that the communication is not outweighed by the interest of the institution in maintaining effective working relationships with constituents and with the efficient provision of education. "A matter of public concern" is defined as something that involves the interests of more than just a few people (Kaplin and Lee 1995). In *Pickering v. Board of Education* (1968), the U.S. Supreme Court held that a school teacher could not be dismissed on the basis of speech on an issue of public concern, absent proof that he or she had recklessly or knowingly made false statements (Hiers 1995; Olswang and Fantel 1980). As a general rule, cases like *Pickering* involving public employees extend to higher education settings, even though academic freedom in elementary and secondary school classrooms and the protection afforded to college and university researchers and teachers are different (Hiers 1995; Lovely 1991).

Whether faculty activities and interests are protected is subject to a three-stage analysis, ending at any stage where a negative answer occurs (Kaplin and Lee 1995). The first stage is a determination about whether the activity is a matter of public concern. The second stage is whether the interest of the individual in engaging in an activity outweighs the interest of the institution in preventing the activity. The third stage is whether the institution would have taken adverse action against the faculty member even without the activity's being involved (Lovely 1991). The decision of the U.S. Supreme Court in *Connick v. Myers* (1983) could represent an emerging view according greater weight to the need of public employers to maintain discipline and harmony in the workplace (Olivas 1993).

Like other rights derived from constitutional principles, academic freedom is not absolute (Riley 1993). As a general rule, institutions can avoid judicial invalidation of their actions in academic freedom cases if strong and dispositive grounds exist for an action independent of matters involving academic freedom. Administrators should consult with counsel before taking any adverse personnel action in response to any form of faculty expression (Hiers 1995). If the speech in question is reasonably likely to pose some imminent risk of harm to institutional operations, institutions may request that the speaker refrain from such speech. Such a request is appropriate, however, only when the speech presents some *real* likelihood of actual interference with the academic enterprise, not simply when the administrator disagrees with the content. Adverse personnel actions based on expression often result in litigation, underscoring the importance of maintaining adequate documentation of language used by administrators in dealing with these situations and the ability to demonstrate actual interference with institutional operations.

Performance evaluations, post-tenure review, and comparable worth
Performance evaluations serve several functions, including the legal function of providing a record that can be used to support positive personnel actions, such as promotion and increases in compensation, as well as negative actions, such as

demotion, discipline, or termination (Benedict and Smith 1992; Carkeek et al. 1988). Evaluations should be conducted according to a common set of criteria, which should be written, clear, specific, and objective. They should also be relevant to different types of employees and applied to them consistently (Copeland and Murry 1996). Neither the criteria themselves nor the manner in which they are applied may discriminate against any employee or group of employees (Craver 1990).

To minimize legal exposure in the context of performance reviews:

- Evaluations should be limited to the duties and responsibilities of the given position. Factors such as lifestyle, religious practices, and other non-job-related conduct are not appropriate subjects for the evaluation. In addition, all aspects of the position should be included in the evaluation. For example, if service is listed as an evaluatory category for faculty, an evaluation that fails to give credit for service is deficient.
- Evaluations should relate to current actions. Recent contributions should not obscure an overall lack of achievement, just as past achievement should not cause the evaluator to overlook inadequate recent accomplishments (Copeland and Murry 1996).
- Evaluations should be conducted by academic administrators trained in the basics of personnel evaluation who understand the fundamentals of employment discrimination law as well as institutional, schoolwide, and departmental criteria (Copeland and Murry 1996; Sarchet 1995).
- It is important to prepare a formal report for each employee evaluated and to have the employee sign the report to signify that he or she reviewed it. Employees' access to their own personnel file may be guaranteed by state statute (Sarchet 1995). It is critical, however, that personnel reports remain confidential. They should be circulated only on a need-to-know basis, both to protect the privacy of the employee and to avoid a defamation action in case the report contains erroneous negative information. Reports should include an account of strengths and weaknesses, suggestions for correcting weaknesses and a time frame for effecting them, and specific and valid reasons for any adverse recommendations.

- An effective and objective appeal process should be available. Under the principle of comity, courts will usually require that a person bringing a complaint exhaust all administrative remedies before applying to a court for relief. Courts will, however, accept cases before all administrative procedures are exhausted if available administrative remedies are inadequate.

Although reviews of probationary faculty to determine their congruity with standards required for tenure are typically mandatory, tenured faculty typically are not evaluated (Burg 1995; Olswang and Fantel 1980). At institutions that have developed a system for post-tenure review, performance criteria currently used in tenure decisions should be applied to tenured faculty being reviewed, providing credit for teaching, research, and service activities within the context of institution- and department-specific standards (Craver 1990). As with any evaluation, criteria may not discriminate (Copeland and Murry 1996). Even if the criteria seem neutral, if performance evaluations of older faculty are consistently below those of younger faculty, the potential exists for a successful disparate impact case under the ADEA (Craver 1990).

Moreover, any termination resulting from a series of negative post-tenure reviews would have to provide process consistent with any for-cause dismissal of a tenured faculty member (Copeland and Murry 1996; Craver 1990; Olswang and Fantel 1980; Sarchet 1995). And although courts display the traditional deference to academic decision making in the context of performance evaluations, judges are more likely to uphold a dismissal if it is the product of a system of evaluation linked with regular faculty development, as opposed to a summative, sanctions-based approach (Burg 1995; Copeland and Murry 1996).

Finally, gender-based wage discrimination is a potential issue in higher education (Luna 1990). Under the theory of disparate treatment, a single plaintiff or class of plaintiffs would demonstrate comparable worth—equal pay for equal work—using statistical evidence (Luna 1990).

Employee misconduct
Institutions and individuals may be held liable for several types of misbehavior that can occur in a department or

school. One area of potential liability is sexual harassment, which is a violation of Title VII as well as the laws in many states that may provide even greater protection (Allen 1995; Keller 1988). Title IX may also be applicable in sexual harassment cases, particularly for students who bring actions (Keller 1988; Roth 1994).

Sexual harassment is defined under Title VII as unwelcome sexual advances, requests for sexual favors, or other verbal or physical conduct of a sexual nature, provided one of three circumstances is present:

- Submission to the conduct is made a condition of employment, either explicitly or implicitly;
- Submission to or rejection of the conduct is used as the basis for decisions about employment; or
- The conduct has the purpose or effect of substantially interfering with performance of work or of creating an intimidating, hostile, or offensive environment (R. Adler and Peirce 1993; Allen 1995; Carkeek et al. 1988; Carroll 1993; Perry 1993; Radford 1994).

Thus, the courts recognize two different forms of sexual harassment: *quid pro quo* (employment conditioned on submission) and *hostile work environment* (Allen 1995; Ciesla 1994; Floerchinger 1995; Keller 1988; Larson 1992; Martell and Sullivan 1994; Perry 1993; Roth 1994). Finally, sexual harassment is not gender-specific, as both men and women can be the target of the harasser.

The issue in sexual harassment cases is not whether the conduct is consensual or voluntary, but whether it is unwelcome. Even if a target appears to be in a consensual relationship, it may be unwelcome and thus sexual harassment (R. Adler and Peirce 1993; Allen 1995; Larson 1992; Martell and Sullivan 1994; Radford 1994; Roth 1994). In other words, a relationship that appears consensual may not actually be so if it is unwanted by the target of sexual harassment. The often difficult question of whether conduct is actually unwelcome is a question of fact to be determined by the court based on the evidence presented by both sides (Radford 1994).

The courts examine conduct from the perspective of a reasonable person in the same or similar circumstances as the subject of the harassment (R. Adler and Peirce 1993;

Allen 1995; Carroll 1993; Ciesla 1994; Leland 1994; Martell and Sullivan 1994; Perry 1993; Radford 1994; Roth 1994). In sexual harassment cases involving women, a serious risk exists that women who are offended or intimidated by sexist conduct will be deemed "unreasonable" according to prevailing male standards. In other words, a pervasive understanding often exists within organizations and institutions that sexual harassment is a harmless amusement to which women overreact and about which they lack a sense of humor. Thus, in sexual harassment cases involving women, the appropriate and applicable standard is that of a reasonable woman (R. Adler and Peirce 1993; Leland 1994).

Institutions are liable in a sexual harassment–based lawsuit if their employees or agents knew or should have known of the offense (Allen 1995; Elza 1993; Perry 1993; Roth 1994). Lawsuits may be brought under a tort theory, such as battery, assault, infliction of emotional distress, defamation, or false imprisonment, or as a wrongful termination (Allen 1995).

Institutions are legally obligated to investigate complaints of sexual harassment promptly and take appropriate disciplinary action when necessary (Carkeek et al. 1988). Therefore, it is critical that institutions establish concrete policies on sexual harassment, increase awareness of the issue across the university community through effective dissemination of information, and encourage academic administrators to enforce the rules defined. Most institutions have a specific policy on sexual harassment. Some have different policies and procedures for students and employees. Some institutions incorporate sexual harassment complaints into existing grievance procedures, and some have established separate processes (Carkeek et al. 1988). Whatever form they take, well-crafted policies and procedures include means for the informal resolution of complaints, as well as due process protections for both parties when informal resolution is not feasible or fails (Carkeek et al. 1988; Carroll 1993).

Formal procedures should:

- Be tailored to the institutional environment;
- Identify campus members who fall under the policy;
- Delineate the nature and range of discipline;
- Describe prohibited conduct, including clear definitions and examples of sexual harassment;

- Outline procedures to file complaints;
- Designate the office to receive complaints;
- Provide for confidentiality to the fullest extent possible; and
- Establish time frames for actions (Allen 1995; Carroll 1993; Ciesla 1994).

Procedures typically include a deadline—usually of approximately 180 days—within which complaints can be filed (Carkeek et al. 1988; Carroll 1993; Ciesla 1994).

Questions may arise over who should investigate a complaint. The answer often depends on the nature and extent of the allegations. The only constant is that the investigator or investigators—whether academic administrators, human resource personnel, or an attorney—must be both impartial and familiar with institutional policy and procedure (Allen 1995). Issues relevant to an investigation might include:

- Identifying the harassing behavior and where it occurred;
- Ascertaining the response of the subject, the presence of any witnesses, whether the conduct was part of a pattern, and what could have been done to stop the behavior; and
- Determining how the situation could be resolved (Allen 1995; Carkeek et al. 1988; Oh 1992).

Sexual harassment policies are usually attentive to issues of confidentiality, both related to filing complaints and resolving them (Ciesla 1994). Although it is not always possible to maintain confidentiality, given the nature of certain offenses (Allen 1995), it is prudent to guarantee against retaliation on the basis of a sexual harassment complaint (Ciesla 1994). Under all circumstances, administrators and others involved in complaints should maintain complete written records of all interviews, investigations, and determinations (Allen 1995). Above all, academic administrators should not treat complaints as necessarily unfounded or frivolous. They should investigate, document, and resolve matters whenever knowledge or allegations of harassment arise and should do so as promptly as possible (Allen 1995). Some cases—such as offensive cartoons or nude photographs posted within offices or classrooms—do not require an investigation before actions can and should be taken to halt the conduct (Allen 1995).

In the context of employment, sexual harassment also takes several forms:

- Quid pro quo harassment might involve a supervisor's asking an employee to have sex with him or her in exchange for a promotion. Moreover, the preferential treatment of subordinates who consent to sexual requests is a form of harassment toward the co-workers who do not (Allen 1995; Larson 1992; Radford 1994; Roth 1994).
- Public displays of nude or seminude pinups, and demeaning or offensive photographs, cartoons, and graffiti in the workplace are examples of sexual harassment in a hostile environment (Allen 1995; Carroll 1993; Larson 1992). The same is true of imposing sexually provocative or suggestive dress codes on employees. In addition, observing the harassment of others can also constitute sexual harassment relative to the observer. The harassment can be so offensive, demeaning, or disruptive as to constitute a hostile work environment, even if it is not specifically directed at the observer (Allen 1995). Similarly, retaliation against an employee for exercising his or her right to stop sexual harassment is prohibited.
- Verbal harassment—stating that a person is not equipped to do a certain job on the basis of his or her gender—is sexual harassment, as are repeated sexist, demeaning, or derogatory jokes or comments, unwelcome comments on appearance, and the habitual use of patronizing or demeaning terms (such as "sweetie" or "babe") (Allen 1995). The same is true of such behaviors as leering or ogling (Allen 1995).
- Physically blocking access to a work area or physically preventing passage through corridors, when the conduct is directed at someone based on gender, constitutes harassment. The most egregious forms of battery and assault—as well as rape and stalking—may be both sexual harassment and violations of criminal law (Allen 1995).
- One form of harassment is repeatedly asking a co-worker on dates after expressed or implied denials, provided the pervasiveness of the request interferes with the ability of a reasonable person to do his or her job. A single request for a date made in a usual manner and context is not sexual harassment just because it occurs in the workplace, however. A single or isolated event of this type is rarely considered severe or pervasive enough to constitute sexual harassment (Allen 1995; Larson 1992; Radford 1994). Under the decisions of the U.S. Supreme Court in *Harris*

v. Forklift Systems (1986) and *Meritor Savings Bank v. Vinson* (1986), sex-based harassment must be sufficiently severe and pervasive to alter the conditions of the work environment and create a hostile environment (Martell and Sullivan 1994).

The bottom line is that voluntary participation in sexual or other acts does not mean they do not constitute sexual harassment, because differences in power often make it difficult to say "no" (Allen 1995). The standard is rather that a reasonable woman or man in the place of the target would feel pressured.

Sometimes issues of sexual harassment arise in the context of consensual relationships between faculty and students (Allen 1995; Keller 1988). When students complain of sexual harassment involving faculty as teachers or advisers, harassment often becomes linked with core academic values, such as academic freedom, free association, free expression, and privacy, and thus can become especially tricky. Some institutions also have specific policies that forbid consensual amorous relationships between faculty and students (Keller 1988). Quid pro quo cases—as with exchanging sex for grades—are more straightforward than less direct forms of sexual harassment, such as unwanted or inappropriate attention directed toward a student (Perry 1993). Inappropriate attention may take several seemingly innocuous forms—invitations to lunch, personal comments on papers, personal notes, personal gifts. Indeed, these less direct cases of harassment are often framed as "special" attention to a "special" student within the context of regular academic life (Allen 1995). What is constant is that the student may feel pressure to accept, given the power of the professor over the student's academic progress. Whether or not the student consents to the relationship, directly or indirectly, is not the issue. The issue is whether a reasonable person in the place of the student would feel pressured.

Further, other indirect forms of sexual harassment occur at universities and colleges—leering or staring at students on campus, using crude or inappropriate language relative to students in jokes or comments in class, commenting that a student of a particular gender should not be studying a particular discipline. Unsolicited and unwanted touching, including hugging or pats on the shoulder, can also constitute sexual harassment of a more direct form and may also amount to the tort of battery (Allen 1995).

Academic administrators addressing complaints from employees or students must balance academic tradition with the prevention of sexual harassment. For example, in investigating and disciplining tenured faculty members, academic administrators must respect the procedural and legal rights associated with tenure. At the same time, the failure to reasonably investigate and discipline offenders in a timely way can result in litigation and liability (Allen 1995; Carroll 1993; Larson 1992).

Thus, the existence of a sexual harassment policy alone is not sufficient to insulate an institution from liability if it fails to properly invoke that procedure (Martell and Sullivan 1994). Moreover, institutions will be held liable for the failure to have an effective policy. Regardless of whether a policy exists or it is effective, if the institution knew or should have known about the harassment—either by employees or nonemployees—liability may result from the failure to take effective action to stop it (Allen 1995; Ciesla 1994; Roth 1994). In addition, an academic administrator, as supervisor, may also be held liable for failing to investigate a complaint or allowing a known condition to persist (Allen 1995; Perry 1993). Thus, not only the person accused of the harassment can be held liable, but also the institution and administrators who failed to act.

Internal sanctions or remedies resulting from complaints of sexual harassment typically vary with the severity of the act. Penalties might range from exacting a promise not to commit the offensive act again, giving a written or verbal warning, or requiring a private or public apology. They might also involve transfer, reassignment of duties, withholding of pay increases, suspension, demotion, and dismissal. Some form of mandatory counseling may also be included (Carkeek et al. 1988; Carroll 1993; Elza 1993). Liability may be found under discrimination laws, tort laws, or even criminal laws in egregious cases. Remedies in civil cases may include compensatory damages, attorneys' fees and court costs, and punitive damages (Allen 1995; Ciesla 1994; Larson 1992; Roth 1994).

In the end, preventing sexual harassment may best be achieved by raising the subject publicly and frequently to sensitize all concerned to the issue (Carroll 1993; Roth 1994). It is also essential to develop appropriate sanctions that mem-

In the end, preventing sexual harassment may best be achieved by raising the subject publicly and frequently to sensitize all concerned to the issue.

bers of the university community know will be enforced. Deans and chairs should express their strong disapproval of behaviors and practices that may be reasonably construed as sexual harassment (Roth 1994).

Deans and chairs must sometimes address forms of misconduct by employees other than sexual harassment, such as violations of the criminal law. Generally, the standard for dismissing employees for alleged misconduct is whether "good cause" exists (Hirschfeld 1995). In other words, to terminate an individual for alleged misconduct, the employer must make a good faith determination that sufficient cause exists based on reasonable grounds (Hirschfeld 1995). The key point in a good-cause determination is often whether the criminal misconduct has a direct nexus to the employment relationship, as with cases involving theft of university property or assaults while on duty. These cases illustrate grounds for immediate dismissal (Hustoles 1995). More difficult cases are those that involve criminal conduct off duty and off campus where the connection to employment is less clear. Similarly, lesser criminal matters may not merit dismissal but may instead be cause for discipline.

In any event, it is critical that academic administrators ensure due process requirements are met whenever considering discipline or dismissal (Hustoles 1995). Due process requirements vary according to the case but generally require some notice of charges and some opportunity to be heard by an impartial decision maker (Hustoles 1995).

Finally, actions based on misconduct by employees may involve the school or department in formal grievance procedures. These procedures exist on most campuses to allow employees to bring complaints; they are generally contained in institutional rules and regulations or collective bargaining agreements (Estey 1986). Grievance processes are credible only when they protect employees from reprisals and involve a decision maker perceived by all to be impartial (Carkeek et al. 1988). Procedures usually involve a series of steps, beginning with documentation of the specific complaint and expected relief and continuing through some sort of investigation and resolution. Grievance procedures typically include time limits for each step and provisions to ensure confidentiality. Policies often exclude certain individuals (for example, student employees) or certain subjects (such as benefits or salary). Some processes allow for employees to be represented before the panel by a third party (Carkeek et al. 1988; Samit 1993).

Defamation
Another area of potential misconduct in the context of employment is defamation. Successful defamation claims allow plaintiffs to recover damages for false statements that cause harm to their reputations (Bazluke 1996; Traynor 1990). Defamatory statements are either libel (recorded defamation) or slander (spoken defamation) (Bazluke 1996). Individuals can be held liable for defamation when they meet four standards:

- The statement at the basis of the claim must be false;
- Some sort of publication—dissemination of the information—must have been made to an identified third person;
- The publication must cause some injury, however nominal, to the person making the claim; and
- The falsehood must be attributable to some fault by the individual who publishes the allegedly defamatory information (Bazluke 1996; Kaplin and Lee 1995; E. Smith 1989).

Even if these standards apply, a defense to a defamation action based on privilege may be used. For instance, statements made in the proper discharge of a legal duty, as well as those made in the context of a legislative or judicial proceeding, are the subject of an absolute privilege, even though they may be made with knowing or reckless disregard for the truth (Traynor 1990). A qualified privilege exists between persons who have a common interest in the subject matter of the expression at issue, as with communication between two people in the context of an organization (Bazluke 1996). The qualified privilege is often invoked in defamation actions in higher education stemming from performance evaluations, terminations for cause, and references for employment. In the case of employment evaluations, courts generally will apply the qualified privilege only if:

- The evaluation was written by the appropriate institutional official;
- The disputed communication was relevant to the employment issues reviewed; and
- The official conveyed the evaluation only to those with a legitimate interest in it (Bazluke 1996).

The standard for what constitutes defamation is different for different types of plaintiffs. In the case of a public figure, the person accused of defamation must show actual malice. Public figures are individuals who have achieved fame or notoriety, including those in elected or appointed public office (Bazluke 1996). For a private figure, the standard is negligence by the person making the statement (Traynor 1990). No specific rules designate who is a public figure and who is a private figure, but a substantial body of case law on the issue is instructive. It seems clear that a university chancellor or college president will be held to be a public figure. For other academic administrators, including deans and chairs, the standard is less clear. Sometimes courts have applied the public figure doctrine and sometimes not (Bazluke 1996). Recovery in defamation cases depends on several factors and may include both compensatory damages for actual losses and punitive damages to punish the defendant and deter similar conduct.

Finally, academic administrators should take precautions against defamation (Bazluke 1996). Regarding personnel files, employers should:

- Maintain documents that are self-substantiating or readily subject to verification;
- Limit access to files to those with an objectively sustainable "need to know"; and
- Disclose documents according to a policy developed in consultation with counsel.

In the area of employment references, academic administrators should exercise care that references:

- Come from the appropriate official, particularly one who has not had a history of interpersonal conflict with the subject of the reference;
- Include only statements that are true and can be verified;
- Avoid gratuitous, subjective evaluations of character or personality; and
- Are copied for files and maintained to ensure confidentiality.

Dismissal and Retirement of Faculty and Staff
Provisions for the dismissal of faculty are usually contained in institutions' rules and regulations. As a rule, institutions can dismiss *tenured* faculty under only two sets of circum-

stances. The first occurs when adequate cause exists based on one of four grounds: incompetence, immorality, neglect of duty, or insubordination (Copeland and Murry 1996; Kaplin and Lee 1995). The second is as a result of program reductions in the context of a bona fide financial exigency.

Nontenured faculty can generally be dismissed provided the dismissal is not based on some impermissible ground, such as discrimination or retaliation for asserting some right guaranteed by law (Kruft 1996; Olswang and Fantel 1980). The traditional legal principle in settings outside tenure is that an employment contract is of indefinite term and terminable at the will of either party. With the erosion over time of the at-will concept, however, legal challenges by dismissed staff and nontenured faculty are increasingly decided within the framework of adequate cause (Hustoles and Doerr 1983–84).

Dismissal of tenured faculty: For cause and financial exigency

In *Board of Regents v. Roth* (1972) and *Perry v. Sindermann* (1972), the U.S. Supreme Court distinguished between the rights afforded faculty members who do have tenure and those who do not, treating nonreappointment of term faculty differently from termination of tenured faculty for cause in terms of the due process rights afforded each group (Copeland and Murry 1996; Olswang and Fantel 1980). Nevertheless, something like tenure may be implied by certain types of employment relationships, as in *Sindermann,* where reasonable expectations of continued employment constitute a property interest. In these "de facto" tenure cases, institutions are responsible for providing adequate protection of the right to continued employment through appropriate due process (Olswang and Fantel 1980).

When property and liberty interests are at issue—as in the case of the dismissal of a tenured faculty member—procedural due process requirements are heightened. These procedural due process protections ensure that tenured faculty are not dismissed as punishment for the exercise of unpopular intellectual pursuits protected by academic freedom (Olswang and Fantel 1980). In *Roth* and *Sindermann,* the Court held that procedural safeguards are required when institutional policy and practice support a claim of entitlement to a position and when the dismissal has the potential to seriously damage the reputation of the faculty member and cause a stigma with an impact on future employment (Kruft 1996). In cases where dismissed faculty suffer a sufficient loss of reputation, the dismissal amounts to a loss of liberty.

When sufficient issues of liberty and property are connected with a dismissal, due process protections typically require adequate notice and a full adjudicatory hearing, usually with the right to counsel and before a tribunal that is both impartial and has academic expertise. In practice, the hearing is frequently before a faculty committee that makes findings of fact and recommendations to the institution's president and board (McHugh 1973). Adequate notice requires explanation of the dismissal in sufficiently full detail to enable the faculty member to identify any error that may exist. Notice should also identify potential witnesses and the nature of their testimony (Olswang and Fantel 1980). Finally, public institutions may be subject to state statutes or administrative regulations regarding due process, while private institutions are commonly subject only to contract law.

Nevertheless, the decisions in *Roth* and *Sindermann* reiterate the general reluctance of courts to substitute their judgment for administrative decisions made within established rules or according to the terms of contracts at educational institutions (Olswang and Fantel 1980). Indeed, no general definition exists of what adequate cause is in the context of the dismissal of a tenured faculty member. The AAUP has chosen to defer to individual institutions, and courts have been reluctant to establish a definition in deference to the professional judgment of academic administrators and faculty committees (B. Brooks 1995). Institutional standards here must be especially clear, however.

Although any definition of the adequate cause required for dismissal must be clear, it need not anticipate or delineate all types of conduct. Institutions need only make every effort in their policies and procedures to include definitions that will be important in the adjudication of any later disputes arising from the dismissal (Kaplin and Lee 1995). Further, at public institutions, standards must avoid vagueness under the Fourteenth Amendment and overbreadth under the First Amendment. Finally, standards must allow for adequate interpretation of the contract at both public and private institutions.

The classic misconduct that amounts to adequate cause is some combination of incompetence, immorality, neglect of duty, and insubordination. These standards are difficult to define, much less substantiate through evidence. In addition, given the justification of academic freedom for tenure—as well as the contractual basis of the tenure relationship between faculty members and institutions—removing tenured faculty members is inherently difficult. But without arduous standards for dismissal, tenure would be a hollow protection for faculty (B. Brooks 1995).

The determination of adequate cause can be made only by the academic peers of the faculty member in question in light of the general customs of both the particular institution and the academic community as a whole (B. Brooks 1995). In the consideration of incompetence, a two-part process is suggested for determining whether termination proceedings should be brought against a tenured faculty member (B. Brooks 1995). First, the tenured faculty member must exhibit a manifest inability or unwillingness to contribute to the dissemination or advancement of knowledge through effective teaching, research, or service. A complete failure in one of these areas is required. In teaching, for instance, a faculty member might habitually be absent from class, employ unacceptable testing practices, prepare and deliver disorganized and irrelevant lectures, not stay current in teaching techniques and the substance of a discipline, and fail to make requirements for the course clear to students (B. Brooks 1995; McGee 1993). Thus, incompetence may be linked with neglect of duty as well as with insubordination and perhaps even immorality. Second, the inability or unwillingness must be apparent for a long enough period that improvement is unlikely. In addition, unless the faculty member's inadequacy or indifference is so egregious that rehabilitation through professional development is improbable or impractical, institutions must attempt remedial measures. When that step clearly fails, then instituting the dismissal of the tenured faculty member can become the appropriate recourse.

Cases of insubordination and immorality (also known as "moral turpitude") usually are more straightforward. Courts have defined insubordination as the failure to follow reasonable requests of administrative personnel (B. Brooks 1995). Moral turpitude is commonly exemplified by the professor who makes improper sexual advances toward a student (B. Brooks 1995; McGee 1993). It may also involve dishonesty, such as research fraud or misrepresentation of credentials, or even extreme vulgarity (McGee 1993).

Given the substantial contractual and legal protection that tenure affords, it is important to remember that the misconduct at issue must be extreme. Insubordination and immorality are adequate cause to dismiss a tenured faculty member only if the determination by the institution of adequate cause on these grounds is divorced from issues of academic freedom. Manifest insubordination is adequate cause because of its potential to disrupt the academic environment, just as making inappropriate sexual advances toward students is potentially destructive to the learning environment.

When institutions dismiss tenured faculty as a result of reduction or elimination of programs, they must clearly demonstrate that a bona fide financial exigency exists. One court defined financial exigency as a demonstrably bona fide and imminent financial crisis that threatens the viability of an institution or program that cannot be adequately alleviated by means other than a reduction in the employment force (Dixon, Lynch, and Swem 1987). Only in such circumstances can an institution exercise the authority implied under academic custom and usage to close programs and terminate faculty, including tenured faculty (Kaplin and Lee 1995; McGee 1993).

As with for-cause dismissals, the burden of proof is on the employer (Dixon, Lynch, and Swem 1987). Inquiry by the courts will focus on the process the institution used to determine the existence of the financial exigency and on the standards used to determine the need for reductions to certain programs and the decision to involve faculty members (Houpt 1992; Olswang and Fantel 1980). In making these decisions, institutions must neither dismiss all nontenured faculty before terminating any tenured faculty nor base decisions solely on seniority. But they must:

- Identify the academic needs of the program or programs identified for reduction, and of the institution as a whole;
- Consider all alternatives to termination of faculty;
- Protect advances resulting from affirmative action programs; and
- Recognize legal prohibitions against age discrimination (Dixon, Lynch, and Swem 1987; Houpt 1992; Olswang 1983).

Both public and private institutions can terminate tenured faculty upon proof of financial exigency, even if employment contracts are silent on the issue (Olswang and Fantel 1980). The dismissal cannot serve as a pretext for dismissing faculty for reasons other than financial exigency, however, and it cannot be used as a means to subvert academic freedom (Olswang 1983). In other words, the termination must be fostered by necessity and made in good faith. Dismissals cannot be arbitrary or capricious (Houpt 1992; Dixon, Lynch, and Swem 1987).

Dismissals premised on institutional necessity are inherently less personal in their impact than dismissals premised on cause, so liberty is less a factor in the due process equation. The property interest in tenure remains significant, however, and institutions must afford substantial due process protection to tenured faculty identified for dismissal resulting from financial exigency.

Finally, at institutions where AAUP rules have been incorporated, dismissed tenured faculty typically have the right to appeal the decision. In the case of a state law or institutional policy, faculty also commonly have the right to be placed in another suitable unit or have the institution pay to retrain them. Not all institutions, however, have incorporated AAUP rules or are subject to state law.

Dismissal of staff and nontenured faculty
The traditional employment relationship between institutions and staff and nontenured faculty is employment-at-will (Carkeek et al. 1988; McKenna and Cuneo 1995a, 1995b). Challenges to wrongful discharge, however, are increasingly framed in terms of adequate cause, as the at-will rule has eroded somewhat (Hustoles and Doerr 1983–84). Plaintiffs have challenged the employment-at-will doctrine using both contract theories and tort theories, arguing enforceable contractual expectations have been created by:

• Spoken and written assurances, promises, and statements made by supervisors;
• Written policy statements in personnel handbooks and other sources; and
• Institutional customs and practices (Finnie and Finnie 1993; Hustoles and Doerr 1983–84; McKenna and Cuneo 1995a, 1995b).

Institutions have little defense against claims founded in custom and practice, such as arguments that longevity or service or general practices in higher education forbid termination on the grounds of fairness, because no actual agreement exists between employee and employer (McKenna and Cuneo 1995a, 1995b). Certain express provisions also suggest adequate cause requirements in written contracts and other writings, as well as in documents that may be incorporated into the contract (Finnie and Finnie 1993).

To minimize or avoid contract-based wrongful dismissal actions, institutions are advised to take several precautions in personnel matters:

- Deans and chairs, and those under their supervision, should avoid making any statement that implies in any way the formation of a permanent contractual relationship (D. Duffy 1995; McKenna and Cuneo 1995a, 1995b). These statements might include oral assurances of job security during an employment interview or ambiguous letters sent to employees to improve morale (McKenna and Cuneo 1995a, 1995b).
- Contracts should avoid mandatory provisions, such as "shall," "will," or "fair," and instead include more permissive language unless the institution is confident of the ability of its supervisors to follow the policies and conditions stated to the letter. Similarly, contractual provisions should be written in plain language, avoid complicated or unrealistic procedures and requirements, and be reviewed periodically by counsel (D. Duffy 1995).
- Disclaimers in employment applications and personnel handbooks underscoring the at-will nature of the employment are advisable, although a disclaimer does not guarantee at-will status (D. Duffy 1995; McKenna and Cuneo 1995a, 1995b). The same is true of having employees sign a document expressly acknowledging their at-will status, or integration clauses that indicate that the entire employment contract is contained in a document, or set of documents, and employees cannot rely on representations to the contrary (D. Duffy 1995).

- Other techniques—such as probationary periods for new employees or policies requiring a review of dismissal decisions by other administrators trained in employment law—have also proved useful to institutions (Carkeek et al. 1988; Finnie and Finnie 1993; McKenna and Cuneo 1995a, 1995b). It has been suggested, however, that some courts have construed the probationary period as implying that employees can be fired only for cause after the probationary period (D. Duffy 1995). Involving outplacement consultants early in the termination process is also advisable (Finnie and Finnie 1993).

- Supervisors should document all employment actions, but it is important not to overdocument the file of one employee compared with others. Files should never be altered (McKenna and Cuneo 1995a, 1995b).

In addition to contract-based theories, several tort theories also challenge the traditional at-will rule. Despite the increasing popularity of allegations of wrongful discharge based on tort theories, however, proving the stringent elements involved has proved difficult for plaintiffs (Hustoles and Doerr 1983–84; McKenna and Cuneo 1995a, 1995b).

- In abusive or retaliatory discharge cases (also known as constructive discharge), plaintiffs allege that the institution forced their resignation through abusive behavior directed toward them. In other words, working conditions are made so difficult or unpleasant that a reasonable person would feel compelled to resign (Finnie and Finnie 1993; Hustoles and Doerr 1983–84; McKenna and Cuneo 1995a, 1995b).
- Interference with business or contract relations actions alleges that the institution induces a breach of the employment contract by the employee through some wrongful act (Hustoles and Doerr 1983–84).
- Negligent or intentional infliction of emotional distress involves outrageous or extreme behavior directed toward an employee and results in severe emotional distress (Hustoles and Doerr 1983–84; McKenna and Cuneo 1995a, 1995b).
- In cases claiming negligent performance of a contractual obligation, the institution fails to meet a duty of ordinary care in performing a contractual obligation toward an employee (for example, an employer negligently conducts an annual employment evaluation) (Hustoles and Doerr 1983–84; McKenna and Cuneo 1995a, 1995b).
- Some dismissed employees have brought defamation actions, alleging that the reasons stated for the discharge are false (Finnie and Finnie 1993; McKenna and Cuneo 1995a, 1995b).
- In actions founded on the theory of the employer's negligence in hiring, training, retention, and entrustment, em-

ployers are liable if they fail to exercise ordinary care in these activities (McKenna and Cuneo 1995a, 1995b). Examples of an employer's negligence include failure to investigate the background of a prospective employee, failure to hire individuals who are competent and qualified for a job, or fraudulent misrepresentation of the institution and what it will offer to the employee (McKenna and Cuneo 1995a, 1995b).

Courts have also carved exceptions to the general employment-at-will rule to combat certain types of behavior by employers. The exceptions are employers' behaviors that are protected by the at-will doctrine but are contrary to public policy. Examples include employees who refuse to engage in illegal acts, those who insist on performing a duty required by statute, or those who are whistle blowers (Finnie and Finnie 1993; McKenna and Cuneo 1995a, 1995b). Certain federal statutory exceptions also apply to the at-will doctrine, including the National Labor Relations Act, Title VII of the 1964 Civil Rights Act, and the ADEA (Finnie and Finnie 1993; McKenna and Cuneo 1995a, 1995b), and laws in several states have also addressed the at-will doctrine (Finnie and Finnie 1993). Finally, workers compensation issues may be connected with dismissals connected with workers' injuries, and deans and chairs should seek appropriate counsel (Steadman 1989).

The actual process of terminating an individual employee is shown below (see Finnie and Finnie 1993, which also offers several practical suggestions applicable to deans and chairs). Overall, the dean or chair should do everything possible to ensure that the decision is made, announced, and implemented in good faith and on reasonable terms.

- The dean or chair should form a committee of key personnel—including the immediate supervisor, the overall supervisor, a representative of the executive officers of the institution, and a human relations officer, all well versed in employment law—to review the decision to terminate an employee.
- Upon reaching consensus in the committee and obtaining the appropriate administrative approval, the dean or chair, accompanied by the supervisors, should notify the dismissed employee. Staff should be assigned to tell co-

Under the 1986 Amendments to the ADEA, institutions may no longer compel the mandatory retirement of employees at a certain age.

workers about the event as it is happening, usher the dismissed employee from the meeting, and handle internal and external communications with or about the terminated staff member.

- Courts generally recognize two valid reasons for a for-cause dismissal. Academic administrators should frame any termination as (1) unacceptable performance, conduct, or record (manifested in the failure to meet specified standards of performance or commission or omission of specified acts); or (2) institutional necessity (evidenced by the exercise of institutional judgment in good faith by the employer). A general statement of the rationale should accompany the letter memorializing the termination, delivered at the termination meeting.

- Decisions to terminate an employee should be carefully documented. If performance, conduct, or record is the reason underlying the dismissal, the written record should show specific performance standards, measurement of the employee against the standards, demonstrated failure to meet the standards, and opportunity and deadlines to meet the standards accompanied by written communications with the employee. If institutional necessity is the reason, the institutional changes that brought about the decision should be documented in good faith. Academic administrators, however, should take care not to go beyond needed and reasonable evidence necessary to make a case.

- Deans and chairs involved in termination actions should assume that the decision will be reviewed later in an adversarial setting. Institutions are likely to prevail in court if a reasonable person would regard the action as consistent with due diligence, good faith, fair dealing, and institutional necessity, and within the spirit and letter of the law.

It is permissible to offer early retirement incentive packages, provided they are strictly voluntary for employees and do not disfavor employees because of their age.

Mandatory retirement and early retirement incentive packages

Under the 1986 Amendments to the ADEA, institutions may no longer compel the mandatory retirement of employees at a certain age (Craver 1990). It is permissible to offer early retirement incentive packages, provided they are strictly voluntary for employees and do not disfavor employees because of their age (Craver 1990; Loren 1992; Stith and Kohlburn 1992). Packages cannot constitute a diminution of benefits, affect otherwise available benefits, or otherwise disfavor the older worker

(Swan 1992). Incentive plans may incorporate a maximum eligible age, but employers usually offer employees who exceed the age a one-time window of opportunity to participate (Craver 1990; Loren 1992; Swan 1992). Reserving the incentive for those whose retirement serves the economic goals of the institution is also permissible (Loren 1992; Swan 1992).

In short, early retirement incentive packages must conform with the requirements under the ADEA that employment-related decisions—hiring, promotion, rewards, punishments, working conditions, salary, benefits, termination—cannot be based on age or age-based stereotypes (Swan 1992). Older employees may challenge policies or decisions on the basis of disparate treatment theory (age-based criteria) or disparate impact theory (neutral criteria that adversely affect a disproportionate number of older workers) (Craver 1990). Typically included within disparate treatment are attempts by employers to make age a bona fide occupational category and thus exempt under the ADEA (Craver 1990). The preferred approach is to use reasonable factors other than age to differentiate between and among workers (Craver 1990).

STUDENTS IN THE ACADEMIC SETTING

Courts increasingly decide cases involving students using implied contract theories, having generally moved from the traditional doctrine of in loco parentis. Institutions are no longer necessarily assumed to have a parental-type relationship with students. Students are viewed as consumers who have reasonable expectations of institutions in the areas of programs and services. In addition, although the traditional deference to academic decision making persists, courts are ever more willing to intervene in campus disciplinary actions involving both academic matters and disciplinary matters. Typically, the key question in both academic and disciplinary concerns is due process: How much notice and how much process is a student entitled to in a given situation?

Other issues concerning students in the academic setting involve admissions, students' records, free expression, and negligence. Although courts continue to afford broad discretion to academic administrators in the area of admissions, institutions will be held in violation of the antidiscrimination laws and Equal Protection Clause when they act in a discriminatory manner, including in the emerging area of disabilities. Immigration law is also a common issue in admissions. Deans and chairs must also be aware of legislation that governs the confidentiality of students' records as well as constitutional provisions that protect the right of students to organize and express themselves. Finally, negligence-based institutional liability for students is a critical concern for academic administrators.

Contract, Consumerism, and Citizenship

The relationship between students and institutions has changed dramatically over the past three decades, and the courts have played a significant role in the evolution (Cooper and Lancaster 1995; Kaplin and Lee 1995; Long 1985; Reidhaar 1985; Walton 1992). Courts traditionally viewed the relationship between students and institutions as one where institutions were largely in control. Although they have sometimes intervened in disputes between students and institutions, only in recent years have courts heard such cases in large numbers (B. Cole 1991; Gregory 1991; Jennings 1981; Nordin 1981). The law increasingly views students as consumers with expectations of institutions for the acceptable provision of programs and performance of services based on an implied contract (M. Smith and Fossey 1995). Courts have come to recognize higher education as less of a privilege and more of a necessity (Hammond 1978).

The long-standing doctrine of in loco parentis—in which the institution is charged with the rights, duties, and responsibilities of parents in supervising students—essentially had been the relationship between the student and the institution until recently (Burling 1991; Jackson 1991; Long 1985). Perhaps the genesis of the change was the campus unrest that accompanied the protest movements of the 1960s. Not only were rights to expression and assembly at issue, but questions also arose about the relationship between students and institutions (Gregory 1991; Jackson 1991; Reidhaar 1985; Walton 1992).

The U.S. Supreme Court's rejection of in loco parentis in *Dixon v. Alabama State Board of Education* (1961) marked the beginning of the movement away from the doctrine (B. Cole and Lewis 1993; Kaplin and Lee 1995; Price and Andes 1990; Reidhaar 1985). Through a combination of social change, legislation, and other court decisions in the years following *Dixon,* students came to be viewed more as adults (Gregory 1991; Walton 1992). For instance, states passed legislation lowering the age of majority, and the Twenty-sixth Amendment to the U.S. Constitution allowed citizens between the ages of 18 and 21 the right to vote (Hammond 1978).

The resulting relationship between students and institutions with the decline of in loco parentis is contractual in nature (Barr 1996; Cherry and Geary 1992; B. Cole 1991; Jackson 1991; Jennings 1981; Schweitzer 1992; Zirkel and Hugel 1989). Students are now considered consumers of higher education, as opposed to wards of institutions (Davenport 1985; Hammond 1978; Nordin 1981; M. Smith and Fossey 1995). In essence, when the student registers and pays tuition, he or she enters into a contract with the institution. Usually, an actual signed agreement between the sides detailing all of the stipulations is not in effect, so much of the contractual relationship is implied (Davenport 1985; Milam and Marshall 1987; Nordin 1981).

Nevertheless, as with other implied contracts, courts have embraced the logic that an agreement exists between the sides. Students agree to follow an institution's rules and regulations, which are stated in the college catalog, student handbook, or other written documents outlining academic programs and institutional policies. If students fail to abide by the institution's standards and rules, the institution can penalize them, including suspension or dismissal.

On the other hand, in exchange for the student's tuition, the institution implicitly assents to provide the academic programs and support services students need to reach their educational goals (Kaplin and Lee 1995; Nordin 1981; Schweitzer 1992). If institutions fail to provide the stated—and thus promised—programs and services, the student may request changes or sever the relationship with the institution (S. Brown and Cannon 1993). Students may take their complaints before courts to compel performance of these implied contracts (Davenport 1985).

Contracts between students and institutions have a long tradition in higher education for service functions, such as financial aid, housing, and food service. These types of contractual relationships were traditionally one-sided in favor of the institution, protecting the university or college but affording the student little recourse when disputes arose. What has changed is that all relationships between students and institutions—services provided by the institution as well as academic programs—are now understood within the context of contract theory. Contract theory affords students considerable protection through informal and formal processes for resolving disputes related to academic programs, including access to court in more extreme cases (S. Brown and Cannon 1993). Although the traditional judicial deference to academic decisions persists, courts are increasingly willing to hear cases involving students, and students have brought a variety of successful actions against institutions (S. Brown and Cannon 1993; Bunting 1990; Cherry and Geary 1992; Davenport 1985; Reidhaar 1985; Schweitzer 1992).

It is important to remember that contractual protections extend to institutions and students alike. In addition, contract theory is applied in much the same way at public and private universities and colleges (Bunting 1990; E. Cole 1994; Hammond 1978; Jennings 1981; Schweitzer 1992). Both types of institutions provide educational programs and services in exchange for the payment from students and thus are held to the terms of the contract into which they enter with students (E. Cole 1994; Hammond 1978; Milam and Marshall 1987; Nordin 1981).

It is thus imperative that universities and colleges—including deans and chairs—keep their promises. Stipulations in school or department catalogs, handbooks, and brochures can be read as implied contracts with students and have the status of any other contract. Regular audits of these materials are essential to ensure that institutions, schools, and departments are actually doing what they say they are doing. Audits should also ensure that institutions, schools, and departments truly want students to comply with all that is written (Davenport 1985). Standards, representations, and information must be clear and consistent, and reflect the institution's missions and values (Cherry and Geary 1992). In addition, all staff must be apprised of their roles in the contractual relationship between student and institution. Their promises, both written and spoken, can be viewed as part of a contract with students (Bunting 1990; Davenport 1985; Zirkel and Hugel 1989).

All institutions must break promises and alter programs and policies under certain circumstances. In general, courts have sided with institutions when revisions have been deemed reasonable and necessary and students have alleged a breach of contract as a result of the changes (Barr 1996; Davenport 1985; Kaplin and Lee 1995). Nevertheless, institutions should attempt to provide alternatives that will cause the least amount of hardship for students when they make changes. Courts have sometimes found in favor of students when programs have lost accreditation or been terminated for other reasons (Nordin 1981). Institutions are obligated to maintain standards and continue programs. If continuation of a program is impossible or impractical, institutions must arrange for students to transfer to related programs with the least disruption possible. They are also well advised to provide as much notice as possible to students.

In addition, institutions can minimize the likelihood of later legal action related to the closing of a program by inserting disclaimers in the documents they produce and disseminate (Bunting 1990; Tanner 1978). But disclaimers will work only when institutions make changes that are essential to their educational mission, arrange transfers to alternative programs for affected students, and publicize the changes well in advance to the extent possible (Cherry and Geary 1992; Nordin 1981).

Students not only have contractual rights relative to institutions but also have an array of rights and protections under constitutions and statutes. Although the U.S. Constitution does not specifically address education, it has been clear since the decision in *Dixon* that students are citizens and do not shed their basic constitutional freedoms when they enter the academy (Kaplin and Lee 1995; Mager 1978; Milam and Marshall 1987; Price and Andes 1990). Public institutions are state entities and are legally bound to follow federal and state constitutional provisions. Although private colleges are not subject to the dictates of the U.S. Constitution, rights paralleling constitutional rights—particularly in the area of due process—have often been incorporated into institutional rules and regulations (Barr 1996; Cooper and Lancaster 1995). In addition, many state and federal statutes apply to public and private institutions alike (Barr 1996).

Courts have been increasingly more willing to suspend their traditional deference to decisions in higher education when constitutional issues are involved (Walton 1992). Indeed, a range of constitutional rights—expression, association, religion, equal protection, due process—have been prominent in litigation involving college and university students (Kaplin and Lee 1995). Courts are increasingly less willing to automatically support decisions by institutions made in the "best interests" of the student, particularly when these decisions may have interfered with the student's constitutionally protected rights (E. Greenleaf 1978; Gregory 1991; Jackson 1991; Long 1985; Reidhaar 1985; Walton 1992). Accordingly, as in the context of contract theory and educational consumerism, deans and chairs are well advised to review school and departmental policies and regulations to ensure that they do not abridge students' constitutional and other basic rights.

Courts have traditionally avoided intervention in campus disciplinary matters involving academic issues but have long been more willing to hear concerns involving students' behavior.

Misconduct and Discipline

Courts have traditionally avoided intervention in campus disciplinary matters involving academic issues but have long been more willing to hear concerns involving students' behavior (Jackson 1991; Long 1985; Mawdsley 1986; Nordin 1981; Reidhaar 1985; Swem 1987). Courts remain more likely to defer to the decisions of academic administrators on purely academic matters—admissions, grades, recommendations, program requirements, degrees—choosing not to substitute their judgment for that of the experts, provided no evidence suggests that the institution's decisions are arbitrary or capricious (B. Cole 1991; B. Cole and Lewis 1993; Zirkel and Hugel 1989). In other words, if academic administrators follow their own rules, the courts are likely to uphold their academic judgments.

Still, courts are more inclined to hear academic issues than they once were, particularly when issues of discrimination or due process are involved (E. Cole 1994; Mawdsley 1986; Milam and Marshall 1987; Nordin 1981; Price and Andes 1990; Swenson 1995). In addition, contract theory has provided students with an alternative way to challenge academic decisions in several types of situations (Jennings 1981). For instance, students have successfully argued that:

- Courses or programs did not meet representations made in catalogs (Jennings 1981; Nordin 1981);
- Curricula failed to adhere to stated institutional or external standards (Davenport 1985); and
- They graduated without the knowledge or certification necessary for their chosen careers (S. Brown and Cannon 1993).

In matters of behavior, courts are more comfortable making determinations of innocence and guilt, which is, after all, what they do daily in a multitude of contexts (Finaldi 1995; Kaplin and Lee 1995; Mawdsley 1986; Schweitzer 1992; Swenson 1995). In higher education, however, the line between when wrongdoing is academic or behavioral is sometimes difficult to locate. Certain types of academic dishonesty—plagiarism, cheating, misrepresentation—may be classified as either (Mawdsley 1986). Generally, institutional custom determines whether such misconduct is punished in the academic context or within a behavioral framework. Because the courts have ordinarily continued to see academic dishonesty as a disciplinary issue, universities and colleges should probably follow that approach.

Disciplinary action is usually the result of an alleged violation of some institutional rule or regulation. In many cases, these rules and regulations are stated in college materials, but they are sometimes based in the institution's unwritten customs and traditions. The key principle that courts have applied in this area is that students must have access to sources of applicable institutional policies and standards, and these sources must be clear and understandable (Kaplin and Lee 1995). The principle suggests that rules and regulations—even when ingrained in the institution's long-standing customs—should be written whenever possible, most likely in catalogs and handbooks (B. Cole and Lewis 1993).

Even when rules and regulations are written, they will not survive legal challenge as the basis of a disciplinary action when:

- They are so vague or broad that they can be interpreted in many ways (Cherry and Geary 1992);
- They are contradictory within an institution or unit;
- They are extraneous to institutional missions; and
- They are inconsistent with external laws, rules, and regulations.

In the latter case, the institution must take special care to comply with directives that come with government grants and contracts (Cherry and Geary 1992; Davenport 1985; Reidhaar 1985).

Not only must institutional rules and regulations that apply to students be disseminated and clear, but academic administrators must also enforce them consistently and fairly. As a general rule, courts are particularly attuned to situations involving the arbitrary or capricious application of institutional rules and are inclined to decide for students in such situations (Milam and Marshall 1987; Nordin 1981). Similarly, rarely enforced rules are inherently suspect when they are unveiled in a given disciplinary case (Milam and Marshall 1987). In short, deans and chairs need to be consistent in applying and enforcing institutional or unit rules and regulations.

Perhaps the greatest area of potential uncertainty and difficulty in disciplinary actions is due process. Students draw due process rights from institutional rules and regulations at public and private universities and colleges, as well as from the judicial decisions that serve as legal precedent (E. Cole 1994). Institutions' failure to adhere to their own rules can give rise to contract-based actions by students (Cherry and Geary 1992). At public institutions, a set of constitutional due process standards and principles apply (Cherry and Geary 1992; Kaplin and Lee 1995; Schweitzer 1992). The basis of constitutional due process requirements is the presence of a property interest in something, for example, the threat to career opportunities arising from a disciplinary action that calls into question the award of certification or a degree (E. Cole 1994; Milam and Marshall 1987). While the decision in *Regents of the University of Michigan v. Ewing* (1985) underscored judicial deference to academic decisions, it also provided a rationale for the involvement of courts in academic matters when a property interest is involved (B. Cole and Lewis 1993; Milam and Marshall 1987; Schweitzer 1992).

It is generally clear that students are entitled to some notice of the charges against them and some opportunity to present their side of the story (B. Cole and Lewis 1993; E. Cole 1994; Long 1985). The recurring question in cases involving the discipline of students is how much notice and process are due in a given situation. In other words, what level of procedure is appropriate to adequately protect the rights of the accused student and concurrently satisfy a court in the case of legal challenge by the student? Although the amount of notice and hearing due a student in a disciplinary matter is determined case by case, some general principles of due process apply:

- All relevant information underlying a disciplinary matter should be made available to the accused student so that he or she has an appropriate opportunity to respond to any charges and question any facts posed by the institution.
- Proceedings need not resemble a trial, but they should be conducted in a manner that allows the accused student the opportunity to be heard and to challenge any of the information in a hearing.
- Legal counsel are permitted only in more serious matters, such as suspension or dismissal (Mawdsley 1986). When present, counsel are limited to serving as advisers to students. Counsel cannot question witnesses or present a defense.
- Courts are inclined to favor an available and meaningful appeal process for students in disciplinary matters (Mawdsley 1986).

In any disciplinary case, academic administrators should avoid making false statements that cause harm to the student's reputation and possibly lead to a defamation action (Bazluke 1996). Anonymous complaints should be avoided, and charges should proceed only when they are subject to substantiation and documentation (Bazluke 1996). And notice of charges should be issued on as limited a basis as possible. In academic matters, courts will generally recognize a qualified privilege for statements made in the proper context, as with faculty evaluations of students' work in class, but no blanket privilege exists.

Finally, to avoid difficulties with due process, academic administrators should do everything possible to ensure that students understand academic performance criteria in both classrooms and programs. In addition, courts are less likely to interfere with academic evaluations when parallel standards are applied to all students (B. Cole and Lewis 1993; Price and Andes 1990). It is also prudent to notify students of academic deficiencies that might lead to suspension or dismissal when the difficulties first become apparent.

Just as they do with other institutional and unit rules and regulations, academic administrators should regularly review all evaluative standards—grading practices, admission standards, certification requirements, degree qualifications—to ensure that they conform with contractual and constitutional dictates (Tanner 1978; Zirkel and Hugel 1989). Accordingly, in the regular review of disciplinary codes, academic administrators should:

- Actively determine the types of misbehavior they intend to address;
- Make explicit the types of offenses that constitute misconduct;
- Articulate the procedures applicable to types of situations; and
- Indicate the types of outcomes that are possible as a result of the disciplinary process (E. Cole 1994; Davenport 1985; Mawdsley 1986; Saunders 1993).

Admissions and Access
Courts continue to afford academic administrators broad discretion in setting criteria for and making decisions about admissions (Bunting 1990; Hammond 1978; Kaplin and Lee 1995; Tanner 1978). As in the employment arena, state and federal discrimination statues typically apply to public and private institutions, particularly when those institutions receive federal funds for certain types of functions (Hammond 1978). Public institutions are also subject to the Equal Protection Clause of the U.S. Constitution. Objective and consistent decisions about admissions will typically be upheld, provided they are not discriminatory. Moreover, courts generally favor admissions policies that conform with the institution's educational missions and that institutions follow without making regular exceptions (Bunting 1990; B. Cole 1991).

Discrimination

The basic standard in student admissions is the same as in employment: Institutions may not unjustifiably discriminate on the basis of immutable characteristics. Absent a compelling reason, institutions may not base decisions about admissions on factors such as race, gender, age, disability, religion, or citizenship (B. Cole 1991; Kaplin and Lee 1995). Several federal statutes, including the Civil Rights Act of 1964 and the Educational Amendments of 1972, are available for use by applicants in combating discrimination in admissions (Moore and Jones 1978). The Equal Protection Clause of the Fourteenth Amendment is also available at public institutions. In addition, claims based on express or implied contracts apply to both public and private institutions (Kaplin and Lee 1995).

As with other academic decisions, the courts will overturn admission decisions only when reasonable and nondiscriminatory explanations for actions do not exist. Students making a constitutional claim about admissions typically argue that not only has equal protection been violated, but also that problems have arisen with due process. In a due process case, the question of whether a property interest is at stake becomes paramount. In cases involving admission, students may show a liberty interest, but it is difficult to make a case that a property interest exists. Thus, due process requirements are often of limited use in challenges involving admissions.

In general, courts allow certain departures from the equal protection principle that people should not be treated differently because of their membership in a particular group when there is a very good reason to do so. In the area of admissions, these exceptions include:

- Affirmative action policies at both public and private institutions;
- Policies related to religious doctrine at church-related institutions; and
- Private single-sex and single-race universities and colleges (Reidhaar 1985).

Race-based affirmative action programs in admissions are an exception to the general principle of equal protection, justified by the sufficiently compelling societal interest in remedying present effects of past discrimination (Heffernan and Bazluke 1996). Despite recent challenges to the foundation of affirmative action in university and college admissions, the decision of the U.S. Supreme Court in *Regents of the University of California v. Bakke* (1978) continues to be binding legal precedent. Thus, affirmative action programs in admissions remain permissible under the Constitution and antidiscrimination statutes, provided that two conditions are met.

The first condition is that the state have a compelling interest at the basis of the program. The compelling interest is usually framed as a way to remedy the present effects of past discrimination. If an institution has ever discriminated, an affirmative action program is required to overcome any present effects. Focusing merely on the institution's interest in a diverse student body to justify affirmative action is an increasingly weaker proposition.

The second condition permitting affirmative action in admissions is that race cannot be the only factor in a decision about admission; it can be only one of several factors. At the relatively few institutions where several prospective students compete for seats in an entering class, several personal qualities of applicants are considered in making decisions whether or not to admit them. Race can be one of those qualities but only in the same way that other nonacademic qualities—participation in extracurricular activities, having a parent who is an alumnus or alumna of the institution, or the ability to participate in intercollegiate athletics—are considered relevant in the decision. Thus, admissions procedures cannot insulate minority groups from consideration in the same pool with all candidates. In other words, as long as institutions consider minority applications along with all other applications—and do not set aside places or establish quotas—affirmative action programs are permissible (Kaplin and Lee 1995).

The U.S. Supreme Court declined to hear the appeal of the notable decision by the U.S. Court of Appeals for the Fifth Circuit in *Hopwood v. State of Texas* (1996) that overturned the ill-conceived affirmative action program at the University of Texas Law School. The *Hopwood* decision directly questions the precedential value of *Bakke* but is in effect only in the states of Texas, Louisiana, and Mississippi (Garfield 1996; Heffernan and Bazluke 1996; L. Ware 1996). Similarly, the edict by the University of California Board of Regents to effectively end affirmative action applies only in the University of California system. Still, whether the *Hopwood* decision and the California Board of Regents's policy will have a ripple effect across higher education remains an open question. Deans and chairs are well advised to remain aware of changes in this fluid area of the law.

In addition, race-based scholarships have been challenged under the principle of equal protection. In *Podberesky v. Kirwan* (1991), the court held that institutions can award scholarships on the basis of race, provided there are particularized findings of the present effects of past discrimination, that the scholarship program has a legitimate remedial purpose, and that it is narrowly tailored to remedy past discrimination at the institution itself (Baida 1994; Heffernan and Bazluke 1996; L. Ware 1996). In other words, race-based scholarship programs should be as modest as possible to correct clearly demonstrated racial imbalances resulting from past discrimination. Once again, it is incumbent upon deans and chairs to work with affirmative action offices on their campuses to ensure compliance with federal nondiscrimination requirements and recent court findings in this area (Butner and Rigney 1993; Kaplin and Lee 1995; Kaufman 1994).

Another exception to the equal protection principle in admissions is at *private* single-sex colleges. These institutions are exempt from sex discrimination legislation (Title IX) based on the demonstrated utility of unique educational opportunities they offer their students (Kaplin and Lee 1995). Single-sex *public* institutions will run afoul of the Constitution, with the Citadel and the Virginia Military Institute having failed in their attempts to justify male-only admissions policies at public military colleges (O'Neill 1997). These public institutions could not provide sufficient reasons to discriminate in admissions based on gender.

The issue of disability in student admissions is less clear. No quota may exist regarding the number of people with disabilities admitted; further, criteria that have a disproportionate impact on applicants with disabilities are prohibited (Kaplin and Lee 1995). Whether people with disabilities are qualified for positions in certain programs is often an issue, however. A common example is in clinical settings where a disability might disqualify a prospective student from performing the program's requirements. For example, a nursing school might reject sight-impaired applicants on the basis of their inability to perform clinical tasks required of a practicing nurse. Similarly, admissions policies based on age need to have a rational relationship to a legitimate state purpose to conform with constitutional standards.

Finally, antitrust issues sometime arise in admissions, though they are unlikely to occur in a school or a department. The decision in *Goldfarb v. Virginia State Bar* (1975) held that antitrust laws apply to higher education. Two types of problems can arise with antitrust issues. One is a horizontal monopoly, in which a group of entities agree to fix the price of a good at a certain level. For example, the Ivy League schools and MIT—the so-called "overlap group"—encountered difficulties with the Justice Department when they attempted to organize their recruiting efforts to avoid bidding against each other for students. The other type of monopoly—the vertical monopoly—involves a single entity's attempting to corner the market on a type of good. Although this type is less likely to occur in higher education, policies established by the NCAA (National Collegiate Athletic Association) have been challenged based on allegations of restraint of trade (Kaplin and Lee 1995).

Disability

Passage of the ADA in 1990 has challenged universities, colleges, and community colleges to revise institutional policies and reshape the physical environment on campus. The ADA expands earlier civil rights legislation for people with disabilities—namely Section 504 of the Rehabilitation Act of 1973—and provides a legal mechanism under which aggrieved individuals may seek relief (R. Edwards 1994; Gehring, Osfield, and Wald 1994; D. Ryan and McCarthy 1994). The act applies to all public and private postsecondary institutions (B. Cole and Lewis 1993; Kaufman 1994). Although the essential relationship between institutions and students with disabilities did not change with passage of the ADA, the act has both expanded rights and heightened awareness (Raisfeld 1994). What the ADA has done—and promises to continue to do—is to afford access to higher education to an increasing number of students with a wide variety of disabilities (Gehring, Osfield, and Wald 1994).

As in employment, the ADA mandates that institutions make reasonable accommodations to ensure access for students with disabilities who are otherwise qualified for educational programs. In meeting the legal requirements of the ADA, all aspects of an institution—admissions policies, evaluation procedures, physical settings—must accommodate students with disabilities wherever and whenever it is reasonable to do so (Tucker 1996; W. White 1993). In short, institutions must ensure that policies and regulations do not have an unreasonable or unfair impact on students with disabilities and that campus programs and activities are accessible to the extent reasonably possible (R. Edwards 1994; Kaufman 1994; Milani 1996). Moreover, reasonable accommodations should not add hardship to the lives of students with disabilities or draw unwarranted attention to the disability (Scott 1994). The goal of accommodations should be to mainstream students with disabilities, not segregate them in special programs and settings (R. Edwards 1994).

The definition of "disability" under the ADA is broad. The act not only covers disabilities that are readily apparent—ambulation, hearing, and sight, for instance—but also includes less apparent disabilities, include learning and psychological disabilities that can often be more difficult to define. Learning disabilities generally refer to disorders that produce difficulties for students in listening, reasoning, or speaking, as well as in mathematics and reading (Brinckerhoff and McGuire 1994; McCusker 1995). A psychological disability is defined as a persistent emotional or mental illness or psychological or psychiatric disorder that impairs educational, social, or vocational functioning (J. Duffy 1994). Courts are continuing to refine the definition of "reasonable accommodation" and to craft appropriate protections for students with learning and psychological disabilities (R. Edwards 1994; Kaplin and Lee 1995). Breakthroughs in understanding developmental issues involving students with disabilities promise to further encourage the expansion of access and opportunity (Serebrini, Gordon, and Mann 1994; Tucker 1996).

Perhaps the aspect of the ADA and reasonable accommodation that has received the most attention on campus and elsewhere is the requirement that buildings and other facilities be modified to ensure reasonable access. If the cost of modification makes the requirement unreasonable, institutions can seek other solutions to make buildings accessible, but any major renovation projects or new construction must meet ADA codes and conditions (Kaufman 1994; Thrasher 1992). Not all reasonable accommodation for students with disabilities requires what is often expensive physical changes in the campus environment. For instance, changes in where events are held to provide more accessible seating may serve the need to accommodate students with disabilities just as well as structural changes in the old venue.

Another aspect of reasonable accommodation for students with disabilities is the provision of services and tools to allow students with disabilities to better navigate the campus and their studies. Technological advances are providing tools to aid students with a wide range of disabilities (Harris, Horn, and McCarthy 1994; Kaufman 1994). Offices to serve the needs of students with disabilities generally coordinate these efforts on most campuses (J. Brown 1994).

Concerns about disabled students' being a drain on institutional resources and disruptive to the educational environment are typically overstated. While some students with disabilities may need some accommodation to participate in mainstream educational opportunities, the accommodation need not be disruptive on campus or in classrooms. Universities, colleges, and community colleges should address intentional or malicious disruption of institutional life by students with disabilities through established disciplinary systems, provided the processes are the same as for all students and the disciplinary action focuses on behaviors, not disabilities. Institutions cannot discipline students simply because of emotional or physical disorders. Instead, part of the philosophy behind the ADA and similar legislation is to treat students with disabilities like other students to the extent possible (E. Cole 1994).

Finally, institutions may require that students verify their disability when they request an accommodation, but they should take particular care to address the matter confidentially and sensitively (Milani 1996; W. White 1993). Moreover, universities and colleges should establish grievance procedures for students who allege that appropriate accommodations are not being made. Such procedures diminish the likelihood of subsequent litigation.

Institutions have established offices and developed policies generally to ensure compliance with the ADA. Schools and departments should work closely with campus experts on such issues in navigating questions about students with disabilities. Deans and chairs should also consult offices on campus that work with students with disabilities to review their policies and operations and make sure they conform with legal mandates and institutional policies (Rothstein 1994). Staff

Deans and chairs should also consult offices on campus that work with students with disabilities to review their policies and operations and make sure they conform with legal mandates and institutional policies.

development programs should also address issues involving students with disabilities (Rothstein 1994).

Immigration and international students

Three percent of all students enrolled at institutions of higher education in the United States are citizens of other countries *(Chronicle of Higher Education,* Almanac 1996). The percentage of international students on campus has increased in recent years and promises to continue to expand in the future. A complex series of statutes and regulations enforced primarily by the INS and the U.S. Department of State regulate the conditions under which foreign nationals may enter the United States and remain in the country (Kaplin and Lee 1995). Most, but not all, international students are in the United States on a temporary basis to pursue their educational goals. These students are within a special INS classification; special INS classifications also apply to the families of international students when they accompany the student. In addition, certain INS rules cover employment, travel, and academic progress. Generally, international students must be enrolled full time and be making satisfactory progress toward their degree or certificate. They may not work off campus unless it is a direct part of their academic program. Most international students may work on campus, however.

Foreign nationals seeking enrollment at colleges and universities in the United States must secure prior approval from an institution that is certified by the INS to receive international students. It is the institution that determines whether international students meet criteria for admission, but students must first demonstrate a proficiency in English and adequate financial resources to cover expenses (Levitov 1992). Once approved, the institution sends INS Form I-20AB to the student, which the student then uses to gain release from his or her country of origin and admittance to the United States and the institution that issued the form. Each country has its own set of rules and regulations regarding study abroad, but Form I-20AB is the key device to connect the prospective international student and eventual enrolling institution. Once the student is enrolled, institutions are required to keep the INS informed of his or her academic status for as long as Form I-20AB is effective.

Most institutions have an office devoted to international students, which typically manages the bulk of the often complex documentation involving the relationship between the institution and international students. All institutions enrolling foreign nationals must name a "designated school official" (DSO), who is charged with monitoring foreign students' status, is the contact for the INS and other relevant government agencies, and is responsible for ensuring that students and the institution are complying with the immigration laws (Neuberger 1992). The INS has the authority to prevent institutions that have failed to comply with the immigration laws and regulations from enrolling international students (Levitov 1992).

Financial aid

The federal government is the source of much of the financial aid that allows students to finance their educations (Butner and Rigney 1993). Federal support comes with often complex requirements and restrictions on who can use funds and how they can use them. In addition, the tradition of scholarship support from private benefactors has continued. Scholarships often have conditions, ranging from a student's scholastic achievement to membership by the student or his or her parents in a certain group or organization favored by the donor. In contrast, government-supported financial aid typically is based on the student's demonstrated financial need. Thus, a complex set of rules and regulations govern institutions in determining eligibility and making awards (Kaplin and Lee 1995). Accordingly, academic administrators are advised to consult with campus financial aid officers when such issues arise.

Constitutional and statutory issues also arise in the area of student financial aid. Civil rights legislation and affirmative action policies influence federal and state financial aid policies and procedures, as well as conditions governing many private scholarship funds (Heffernan and Bazluke 1996). Within this context, students challenging the denial of aid or its renewal by institutions have increasingly gone to court to settle their differences, using these laws as a basis.

Students' Records

The Family Education Rights and Privacy Act of 1974 (FERPA) (as revised in 1988)—also known as the Buckley Amendment—controls access to students' records (Kaplin and Lee 1995). The act has required academic administrators

---

to confront two key questions in the area of students' records: What constitutes a record as covered by the act, and who can be afforded access to records? The act applies to public and private institutions alike and covers both current and former students (E. Cole 1994). In addition, the act requires that each institution designate an official to monitor students' records and compliance with FERPA. Moreover, state laws on invasion of privacy have some application to colleges and universities and may apply in the context of students' records (Kaplin and Lee 1995).

The intention of the Buckley Amendment is to maintain the confidentiality of students' records, eliminating two types of situations: those where students could not review and challenge damaging and false information in their files and those where anyone interested in viewing a record could obtain access to it. "Students have a right to know what records exist, the content of these records, and their accuracy. Further, they have the right to control releases of the information from these records" (Bracewell 1978, p. 32). Under the act, institutions must provide students access to their own educational records, students may question information in their files, and a grievance process is available to students who desire to make changes or deletions to their records (B. Cole 1991).

Institutions must also protect the confidentiality of students' records. Only those administrators, faculty, and staff with a clear "need to know" can have access to students' records. And these individuals can have access only to portions of the records that pertain directly to legitimate educational purposes, such as student advising, auditing credits taken, or a review of degree requirements. Institutions may provide access to outsiders in only a few cases:

- Accrediting agencies may use certain material in files for research or auditing;
- Parents of students considered dependents under the federal tax laws may have access to information in students' records; and
- A court has ordered it (Van Tol 1989).

Counselors or other staff may have personal notes on certain students that are kept separate from educational records. Institutions must ensure that these notes are kept confidential and are used only in direct personal relationships with the student (E. Cole 1994).

Given these restrictions, staff should be instructed not to release any information about a student—even basic information and even to parents—without assessing the application of FERPA. Until someone with sufficient background in students' right to know and issues of confidentiality has been consulted, all school and department personnel should err on the side of caution by not releasing any information contained in any student record to any person who does not have a direct, legitimate education-related purpose for accessing the record.

Expression, Organizations, and Publications

Like other constitutional protections, the First Amendment applies only to restrictions by public institutions on protected activity by individuals and groups. First Amendment rights are not absolute. Public institutions can impose reasonable regulations on expression and assembly with regard to the time, place, and manner of their occurrence (Jackson 1991). In other words, speech that involves a substantial deviation from the normal activity at a particular place at a particular time can be regulated (Kaplin and Lee 1995).

In *Clark v. Community for Creative Non-Violence* (1984) and *Ward v. Rock Against Racism* (1989), the Supreme Court articulated a three-part test for upholding regulations relating to expression proffered by public institutions. The first part of the test is that the regulations can make no reference to the content of the expression. An example of an inappropriate content-based regulation is to restrict speech to what is a "wholesome nature," as was the situation in *Shamloo v. Mississippi State Board of Trustees* (1980). There are some exceptions to the general principle that content cannot be regulated, however. Speech that lacks any real value—obscenity, fighting words, incitement, private defamation—can be regulated on the basis of content (E. Cole 1994; Jackson 1991). Nevertheless, a public institution may not prohibit speech simply because persons who hear it may be offended by the message.

In addition, "hate speech"—speech or acts that are not intended to communicate ideas or information but only to humiliate or wound through grossly negative assessments of persons or groups based on a classification protected under the discrimination laws—is not protected, but campus regulations on hate speech have been difficult to craft narrowly enough to prevent prohibiting speech involving the exchange of ideas that is protected under the First Amendment (Jackson 1991; Kaplin and Lee 1995; Page and Hunnicutt 1994; Riley 1993). The principle underlying regulations addressing hate speech is that certain types of expression— such as threats or intimidation aimed at particular individuals or groups—take on the attributes of conduct, as opposed to speech, and should not be protected.

The second part of the test is that the regulations need to be narrowly tailored to serve a substantial governmental interest. This requirement responds to the constitutional principles that regulations must be neither overbroad nor vague. The overbreadth principle requires that standards be sufficiently narrowly tailored to avoid sweeping within their coverage activities that would be constitutionally protected. The vagueness standard requires that regulations be sufficiently clear so that persons can understand what is required or prohibited and conform their conduct accordingly.

The third part is that any regulation must leave open ample alternative channels for communication. Prior restraints on speech—decisions made by institutions in anticipation of an event to prevent it based on fear of disruption—are disfavored but are not invalid if they are limited to determining whether an activity will cause a substantial disruption. A substantial disruption, moreover, need not be a fait accompli. Reasonable restrictions on time, place, and manner are permissible. The freedom to protest is not the freedom to disrupt. Nevertheless, institutions cannot base a restriction on protest solely on the fear of protest (Kaplin and Lee 1995).

Student organizations

As a general rule, public universities and colleges must recognize students' First Amendment right to organize, even if the institution disagrees with the purposes of the group (Reidhaar 1985). Under the decision in *Healy v. James* (1972), however, institutions may restrict the rights of students to organize when one of three conditions occurs:

• When student groups are not willing to adhere to reasonable campus rules;

- When the assembly would interrupt classes or substantially interfere with the opportunity of other students to get an education;
- When it would be illegal under federal, state, or local law for the group to assemble.

To satisfy requirements for due process, institutions should provide some reasonable opportunity for the student group denied status to respond to the denial. In addition, once an institution recognizes any student organization, the presumption is that new organizations formed by students will be afforded the same rights and privileges as established ones (Kaplin and Lee 1995).

Institutions can also restrict the use of facilities for religious activities if they are incompatible with their educational mission. The decision in *Widmar v. Vincent* (1981) addressed an institutional regulation that prohibited the use of facilities for religious worship or religious teaching. The U.S. Supreme Court rejected the institution's argument based on the Establishment Clause that to allow the religious group on campus would cause the school to be promoting religion. Instead, the Court adopted a free speech approach, holding that religious groups have a right to petition for the use of campus facilities but that the institution need not:

- Provide forums for religious groups not otherwise generally available to student groups;
- Create a forum if one does not exist; and
- Provide access to facilities that are not part of the forum.

The *Widmar* decision prohibits only content-based restrictions on access, not regulation of all forums or all content. For example, an institution can prohibit content if evidence exists that a religious group will dominate the open forum (Kaplin and Lee 1995). Courts will also draw a line when a student organization has illegal activities as its chief purpose.

The decision of the U.S. Supreme Court in *Rosenburger v. Rector and Visitors of the University of Virginia* (1995) addressed a similar set of issues. In *Rosenburger,* the institution was held to have violated the First Amendment by failing to award funding to a student journal that served religious purposes, again based on the Establishment Clause. The

Institutions can also restrict the use of facilities for religious activities if they are incompatible with their educational mission.

definition that the university applied to religious activities to avoid potential problems with the Establishment Clause—efforts that "primarily promote or manifest a particular belief in or about a deity or an ultimate reality"—was too broad, according to the majority opinion. It would include discussion of philosophers and poets, for instance. Thus, applying the principle in *Widmar,* the Court found that the students involved in the case had the right to form a group based on virtually any subject they wanted and could use student activity fees at a public institution (Morris 1996).

Students also have a right *not* to organize in some cases. Students have successfully challenged mandatory fees collected by institutions and allocated to organizations or publications that are contrary to their beliefs and views, claiming an infringement on their First Amendment rights (Gibbs 1995; Kramer 1995; Morton 1985; Walsh 1994). As a general rule, mandatory student activity fees are allowed only if the group can legitimately claim that it is dedicated to educating students on behalf of the university and not to achieving political or ideological goals to a degree that outweighs their educational value. In other words, when a group becomes a vehicle solely for a particular viewpoint, it is acceptable to disallow mandatory activity fees (Kaplin and Lee 1995).

In short, when public institutions have attempted to suppress certain student organizations, they have routinely been unsuccessful when challenged in the courts (Liddell and Douvanis 1994). Technically, an institution's interests in maintaining the educational environment are balanced with students' rights under the First Amendment. Given the paramount importance of First Amendment privileges, however, the institution must overcome a huge presumption favoring the right of all citizens, including students, to organize and assemble.

Private schools have more latitude in limiting the establishment and recognition of student organizations, but they still must exercise care in these issues (Liddell and Douvanis 1994). In *Gay Rights Coalition of Georgetown University Law Center v. Georgetown University* (1987)—one of the few assembly cases brought against a private institution—the institution attempted to exclude an organization it felt violated its religious tenets. The collective result of several separate decisions in the matter allowed the university to avoid recognizing the group but required it to provide the organiza-

tion with facilities, services, and funding afforded to other
student groups (Kaplin and Lee 1995).

Student publications

Like student organizations, student publications sometimes
have a direct link to academic units. Publications of a school
or department usually are associated with and funded through
student organizations. Campuswide student publications are
often supported by a student activity fee or through the student government. Freedom of the press is the most staunchly
guarded of all First Amendment rights, and student publications at public institutions receive full protection under the
First Amendment. Under the decision in *Papish v. Board of
Curators of the University of Missouri* (1973), First Amendment
protections persist even when what students write is in poor
taste or causes a substantial outcry on campus (Kaplin and
Lee 1995; Reidhaar 1985).

Courts regularly afford student publications at public institutions protections parallel to those enjoyed by newspapers in
general (Kaplin and Lee 1995). Thus, the courts will likely
view unfavorably any attempts by public institutions to control
or influence any student publication, just as attempts by the
government to limit discussion in a city newspaper would be
very unlikely to withstand a challenge based on the First
Amendment. Accordingly, an institution can eliminate or
change funding to an institution-supported student publication
only for reasons wholly unrelated to the First Amendment.
Some noneditorial functions of the newspaper can be regulated somewhat, however, such as prohibiting discrimination
in staffing or setting advertising policies (Kaplin and Lee 1995).

Like all publications, student publications are subject to
laws prohibiting libel and obscenity. Moreover, any advertising cannot be false or misleading, and it cannot propose illegal transactions. Thus, institutions are well advised to encourage student publications to work with faculty or staff
advisers, not for the purposes of control or censorship, but to
encourage responsible journalism. The bottom line is that
control or censorship amounting to prior restraints on expression is disfavored under the U.S. Constitution (Bazluke 1996).

The same First Amendment restrictions do not apply to
private institutions, but institutional rules and implied contractual relationships with students might give rise to some
student rights in the area of student publications. Finally,

institutional liability for defamation in student publications will depend on the degree of control that the institution exercises over the publication (Bazluke 1996).

Institutional Liability

Even with the essential abandonment of in loco parentis, students continue to expect universities and colleges to ensure their safety while enrolled (Burling 1991; Jackson 1991; Kaplin and Lee 1995; Long 1985; McLean 1987; Walton 1992). The expectation is based increasingly on the contractual relationship between students and institutions (M. Smith and Fossey 1995). Courts have held that institutions have a duty to students to reasonably protect them from harm. Institutions may be liable for criminal acts committed against students on campus, and they may be liable for injuries suffered by students while they are engaged in programs and activities, on campus and off (McEvoy 1992; M. Smith and Fossey 1995; Walton 1992). Although claims involving institutional liability commonly occur in the context of student activities, schools and departments may have some connection to a liability dispute because they sponsor an activity.

Courts have often likened the duty of higher education institutions to students in the area of liability to the landlord-tenant relationship (Kaplin and Lee 1995; McEvoy 1992; M. Smith and Fossey 1995). Although landlords have a duty to protect those whom they invite on their property against risk of harm (Burling 1991), courts have steadfastly declined to hold institutions liable for the safety of students in all situations, applying a standard of reasonableness (Janosik 1991; McLean 1987; Walton 1992; Young 1978). Courts have predicated findings of institutional liability on whether institutions knew or should have known about the risk of harm to students (Burling 1991; Kaplin and Lee 1995; McEvoy 1992; Walton 1992). The duty owed to students is one of reasonable care in inspecting premises to discover possible dangerous physical and criminal conditions, and warning and protecting them from foreseeable dangers arising from the use of property (Burling 1991).

Institutional liability to injured students is often a question of the level of involvement between the institution and the activity in question, with greater involvement increasing the likelihood of establishing a duty. In other words, in cases where an institution can demonstrate that it had no real influence over the activity or surrounding that caused the harm to the student, courts are less likely to find the institution negligent. When institutions have a stronger connection—as with harm caused by institutional employees or involving campus facilities—it is more likely the courts will find an affirmative duty to protect students against harm (Janosik 1991; Kaplin and Lee 1995).

Academic administrators should work with risk management staff at their institution to review and minimize possible situations that could trigger claims of institutional liability (Janosik 1991). Anticipating potentially dangerous situations and making the changes possible to alleviate them protects students and institutions alike (Bennett 1990; Burling 1991).

REGULATION AND OVERSIGHT IN THE SCHOOL AND THE DEPARTMENT

Several state and federal regulations influence the administration of higher education. Although most deans and chairs have little direct contact with certain regulatory statutes—federal environmental laws, state sales taxes, or local zoning ordinances, for instance—several other regulations have a substantial effect on administrative decisions in units. For example, decisions about employment and admissions are greatly influenced by laws on discrimination. Understanding other federal legislation—particularly rules and regulations addressing intellectual property, open meetings, family and medical leave, funded research, and taxation—is equally important to the effective operation of academic units. Similarly, schools and departments are typically heavily involved in accreditation issues affecting programs or the institution that are coordinated by private associations. These associations serve a quasi-regulatory function, and it is important that deans and chairs know about them and how they function.

Copyrights, Trademarks, and Patent Law

The copyright laws, specifically the Copyright Act of 1976, provide the author or originator of certain literary works and artistic productions with the exclusive right to reproduce and distribute them for a set period of time. Protection extends to original work in any tangible medium of expression—such as writing, music, drama, choreography, painting, photography, and sculpture—but does not extend to facts or concepts by themselves, only when they have been collected and organized in some meaningful way (Crews 1993; Hemnes, Pyle, and McTeague 1994). Unpublished material has the same protection as published material. It is not necessary that material be registered and contain a copyright notice ("C" in a circle). Thus, users should assume that all works that could be copyrighted are protected under the law (Crews 1995).

With the decision in *Basic Books v. Kinko's Graphics Corp.* (1991), the copyright has surfaced as an issue at colleges and universities (Crews 1993, 1995; Kasunic 1993). The decision brought commercially produced coursepacks—collections of readings taken from various journals and books and assigned to students by professors—squarely under the Copyright Act. Under the decision in *Basic Books,* the producer of a coursepack must obtain prior permission from the publisher of any work that is copied and may have to pay royalties unless the use meets each of the four standards that determine "fair use"

(Kasunic 1993). What constitutes fair use is linked to the specific facts of each situation and can be summarized in four questions (Crews 1995):

- *What is the purpose and character of the use?* Nonprofit education uses are preferred over commercial uses. In other words, when a profit motive is attached to the photocopying, it is likely not fair use and requires permission (E. Wagner 1991). In schools and departments at universities and colleges, the purpose and character of photocopying is generally educational and not for profit. An exception is commercially produced coursepacks, as was at issue in *Basic Books,* where the court found a profit motive by commercial photocopying shops in providing the service.
- *What is the nature of the copyrighted work?* It is generally easier to establish the fair use of a published work than an unpublished work. Moreover, copying a factual work is more likely to constitute fair use than copying a work of fiction, given the presumption in the copyright law favoring the dissemination of ideas (Hemnes, Pyle, and McTeague 1994; E. Wagner 1991). In *Basic Books,* the defendant met only this part of the four-part test.
- *How substantial is the amount of the work to be copied in relation to the work as a whole?* Copyright laws do not set a numerical or percentage limit, and courts have interpreted the standard of "substantial amount" quite differently. Even a small portion of a work may be deemed substantial, however, if it constitutes a central or critical part of the ideas of the original work (Hemnes, Pyle, and McTeague 1994; Kasunic 1993; E. Wagner 1991). *Basic Books* suggests that even a university-run photocopying operation engaged in the production of coursepacks would likely not fall within fair use in most cases—particularly on the substantial amount standard—and would have to get express permission to photocopy each article or chapter used in the coursepack (Hemnes, Pyle, and McTeague 1994; E. Wagner 1991).
- *What effect will the use have on the potential market value of the work?* In *Harper and Row Publishers v. Nation Enterprises* (1985), the U.S. Supreme Court deemed market impact the most important factor in an analysis of fair use (Kasunic 1993). The Court limited fair use to copying

that does not materially impair the marketability of the work being copied (Hemnes, Pyle, and McTeague 1994; E. Wagner 1991). A professor who distributes a significant quantity of copyrighted material in class—which, taken as a whole, might constitute an anthology—should therefore obtain copyright permission for each work.

The four factors are somewhat difficult to apply because they are interdependent (Hemnes, Pyle, and McTeague 1994). For instance, "market value" is related to "substantial portion" because more substantial copying is more likely to have an adverse economic effect on the copyright holder. Nevertheless, even under the ruling in *Basic Books,* including short quotations from published works in a scholarly study or placing a few copies of an article on reserve for all students in a class to share is likely to be considered fair use (Crews 1993, 1995).

The showing of copyrighted videotapes may also be an issue for school or departmental administrators. The activity is permissible under the copyright laws when done within the context of teaching in a classroom at a nonprofit educational institution and the copy of the videotape itself is lawfully made (Hemnes, Pyle, and McTeague 1994). In addition, computer software and standardized tests are also protected under the copyright laws and usually require that institutions follow conditions set out in accompanying site licenses (Crews 1995; Lutzker and Eure 1993–94). Although backup copies and some modification of software are permissible, permission is usually required for institutions to network software (Hemnes, Pyle, and McTeague 1994).

Copyright permission is available for many works through a general bureau established by publishers, the Copyright Clearance Center, or may be obtained through individual publishers. It is important to obtain the needed permission, and most commercial photocopying businesses or campus photocopying services will obtain the appropriate permissions for work requested to be copied. Plaintiffs in copyright infringement actions are entitled to actual damages and lost profits (which are usually minimal in an academic setting) or statutory damages of up to $20,000 set by the court. Intentional infringement is punishable by statutory damages of up to $100,000 (Crews 1995; Hemnes, Pyle, and McTeague 1994; Kasunic 1993; E. Wagner 1991). Finally, any Eleventh Amendment immunity that state institutions might once have had for infringement lawsuits was eliminated by statute in 1990 (Burgoyne 1992).

A patent is different from a copyright. It is the grant from the U.S. Patent and Trademark Office for a period of years that allows the patent holder, in exchange for the full disclosure of the patented invention, to exclude others from making, using, or selling the invention or requires them to obtain a license to do so (Lutzker and Eure 1993–94; Patel 1995; Stopp and Stopp 1992). Something can be patented if it embodies some new idea or principle not before known and patented. The subject of a patent must be an actual discovery, as distinguishable from mere mechanical skill or knowledge.

Determining who owns the patent is an issue that often arises at colleges and universities. Generally, in sponsored research, the question is determined by the funding agreement. If not, ownership is a personal property issue and is governed by state law. Finally, institutions commonly trademark certain symbols—often institutional names or athletic logos but potentially any word, name, or symbol—creating a property right on its use. In its essence, a trademark expressly distinguishes a product, broadly defined, from those produced by others (Lutzker and Eure 1993–94).

Openness and Disclosure

Openness and disclosure in the operation of public institutions is encouraged through open meetings and records laws (also called "sunshine laws") in all 50 states. Legislation governing open meetings provides the right of the public to attend meetings but not necessarily to participate in them (Cleveland 1987). Nearly all public institutions fall within the criteria commonly applied by open meeting acts, typically receiving or spending public money or performing a public function. Open meetings laws raise several questions for universities, colleges, and community colleges that must comply with them. Such questions are resolved differently in each state because of differences in statutory language and intent, as with the question of what part of a public meeting—all discussion, some discussion, or only voting—must be held in the open (Cleveland 1985, 1987).

Internal staff meetings—the type of meeting generally applicable to deans and chairs—are usually not covered under open meetings legislation, and faculty meetings are generally held to be analogous to staff meetings (Cleveland 1985, 1987).

Chance, informal, or social gatherings are generally not subject to the law, unless they are held in anticipation of or in conjunction with a typically covered meeting (like a board of trustees meeting) (Cleveland 1985, 1987). Finally, certain disadvantages often accompany the positives of openness and disclosure at public institutions, specifically a general unwillingness to conduct sensitive matters in public, such as search processes and hiring decisions (Cleveland 1987).

Other state legislation that focuses on openness and disclosure, such as conflict-of-interest statutes and requirements that contracts be the subject of competitive bidding, are likely of little concern to school or department administrators. Some federal legislation has similar aims, as with the requirement that institutions regularly disclose campus crime statistics. Federal and state whistle-blower acts also encourage openness and disclosure by protecting certain employees from retaliation by employers for exposing wrongdoing (Burling and Matthews 1992).

Federal legislation requiring a drug-free workplace may also reach departments and schools, particularly at universities.

Federal legislation requiring a drug-free workplace may also reach departments and schools, particularly at universities. The statute requires applicants for federal funds to certify, as a precondition for the award of contracts or grants, that they will undertake certain steps to prevent illegal drug use in the workplace by employees who are directly engaged in the federally sponsored work (L. White 1989).

Finally, occupational safety and health regulations may involve schools and departments. The federal Occupational Safety and Health Administration is authorized to investigate—with no advance warning—suspected safety hazards and violations of its regulations for all workplace facilities involved in interstate commerce—which includes practically all colleges and universities.

Family and Medical Leave

The Family and Medical Leave Act of 1993 requires covered institutions to provide eligible employees up to 12 weeks of unpaid leave during any 12-month period for:

- The birth and first-year care of a child;
- The adoption or foster placement of a child in the home of the employee;
- The care of a spouse, child, or parent with a serious health condition; and

- The serious health condition of the employee (Flygare 1995).

Covered institutions are those with more than 50 employees, and eligible employees must have worked at the institution for at least 12 months and for 1,250 hours during the previous year (or about 25 hours per week on average) (Flygare 1995). Employees must give 30 days advance notice before taking the leave, if the need for the leave is foreseeable. With some exceptions, employees are entitled to return to the same or an equivalent position at the end of the leave, and to have all benefits unconditionally reinstated. Institutions are required to maintain any preexisting health insurance during the leave, provided the employee pays his or her share of the premiums (Flygare 1995).

Research and Teaching

Legal issues involving research and teaching are common in higher education. One such issue is the ownership of research data. As a general rule, the ownership of original research data, in whatever form it may be expressed, resides with the institution employing the researcher. The logic underlying the rule is that "works-for-hire"—work completed during working hours—should belong to the employer (Fishbein 1991; Lutzker and Eure 1993–94). The regulations governing federally supported research usually permit institutions to retain legal title to the data produced. In other words, institutions can patent, copyright, and license the data produced in the context of research funded by the federal government, as well as control its dissemination and use (Fishbein 1991). Whether graduate student research assistants have ownership of research data is a more open question, as the employer-employee relationship is often less clear (Patel 1995).

Traditionally, institutions permit researchers in their employ to copyright for themselves scholarly articles based on their research data, but the ownership of the actual data remains with the institution. If a researcher is to claim ownership of research data, he or she must claim that the work was done outside the course of employment. In doing so, however, the researcher relinquishes any right to call upon the institution for indemnification or legal defense should the research activities prompt investigation by the government or private litigation (Fishbein 1991). Further, in the area of patents, most universities have established some sort of revenue-sharing scheme between faculty investigators and the institution (Stopp and Stopp 1992). These agreements, as well as issues of the ownership of research, generally prompt universities to require regular reporting of research activity to the institution (Fishbein 1991; Stopp and Stopp 1992).

A related legal issue is whether outsiders can force access to data compiled in the course of academic inquiry, particularly in situations where the collection or analysis of the data is incomplete. Laws and regulations permit the government access to any data generated in the course of government-sponsored research (Fishbein 1991). Similarly, the employment relationship that typically provides the institution with ownership of data usually also includes the right to examine any data, regardless of the source of funding (Fishbein 1991). Indeed, the first step in any allegation of scientific misconduct is for the institution to take possession of relevant research materials to avoid any actual or perceived tampering with the data in anticipation of the investigation (Fishbein 1991).

In deciding whether to allow outsiders—particularly those in the midst of litigation—access to research data, courts have applied a "balance test" that considers:

- Probable probative value of the data;
- Need for the data demonstrated by the party seeking it;
- Risk of harm to the research project from premature disclosure;
- Availability of the information elsewhere; and
- The potential for insupportable burden to the researcher (Fishbein 1991).

The premature disclosure of research data could have several detrimental consequences, including disrupting the scientific peer review process, compromising intellectual property interests, jeopardizing collaboration in research between institutions and industry, and chilling the ability of scientists to pursue research ideas freely (Lewis and Vincler 1994). Federal legislation does not protect the interest of researchers in preventing access to research data, but several states have enacted specific legislative exemptions that protect research documents at public institutions (Lewis and Vincler 1994). Often these protections are part of state public records acts or are contained in the statutes governing public university functions.

A related set of issues in research revolves around the need to retain confidentiality in reporting data. A researcher could be confronted with the dilemma of refusing a court order to reveal the identity of a research subject promised anonymity (Douvanis and Brown 1993). Such cases usually turn on contract theory, with the promise of confidentiality as an offer, the giving of the information as the acceptance, and the volunteering to provide the information as the consideration. The possible consequence of refusing to reveal confidences is being held in contempt of court. If the researcher complies with the court order, he or she is exposed to possible litigation brought by the person whose confidences are exposed. The researcher also faces potential ethical sanctions within the professional community. The only federal legislative protection for researchers against being forced to reveal the identities of anonymous subjects—except in compelling public interest cases—is in the areas of drug and mental health research (Douvanis and Brown 1993). A few states have similar protections.

Another regulated area in research is the rules—federal regulations as well as internal rules at most institutions—protecting animal rights and human subjects in research. Care and use committees are required by federal contracts for research involving animals, and prior informed consent is necessary from human subjects of federally funded research.

Cases of scientific misconduct also arise in the context of research. The primary federal agencies charged with defining, investigating, and prosecuting allegations of scientific misconduct involving federal grants are the National Science Foundation (NSF) and the Office of Research Integrity of the National Institutes of Health. The NSF defines misconduct as fabrication, falsification, plagiarism, or retaliation against another who provides information about suspected misconduct (Parrish 1995). Institutions have the primary responsibility for investigating allegations of scientific misconduct. Possible penalties for misconduct include debarment from receiving federal funds for a period of time (Parrish 1995). The procedures for investigating and deciding cases of scientific misconduct are complicated, and academic administrators are well advised to seek the counsel of on-campus or other experts in the field.

In the area of teaching, state statutes and regulations directed at ensuring proficiency in spoken English among

The primary federal agencies charged with defining, investigating, and prosecuting allegations of scientific misconduct involving federal grants are the National Science Foundation and the Office of Research Integrity of the National Institutes of Health.

classroom instructors may become an issue of concern to deans and chairs. Statutes and regulations vary by state, some covering only teaching assistants and others covering all instructors. In general, the laws require institutions to ascertain proficiency in English by some diagnostic instrument, with the institution required to remediate or correct any unsatisfactory behavior (Olivas and Reyes 1996). The inherent difficulties in legislating proficiency in a language pose real problems on campuses (Olivas and Reyes 1996). Some who would fall within the definition of "proficiency" under some laws, for example, might still be very difficult to understand because of thick accents or soft voices. In addition, such legislation may be discriminatory on the basis of race or national origin, under either disparate treatment or disparate impact theory (Olivas and Reyes 1996). When language screening is done with new teachers, it would be prudent to do it with *all* new teachers, not simply on the basis of an accent, immigration status, or ethnicity (Olivas and Reyes 1996).

Taxation and Fundraising
Higher education institutions are typically exempt from federal and state taxes. The traditional justification for the exemption is based on the benefits that education provides for communities; the exemption is quid pro quo for the service higher education provides to society. In other words, the tax exemption is essentially a payment by the people of the state for the social good that the institution brings them. Institutions must still pay social security taxes (except for students and visa holders) and unemployment compensation taxes, however. In addition, scholarships and fellowships are taxed, with the portion used for books and tuition exempt. Student housing and compensation for teaching are also not exempt.

Another issue involving taxation—one less likely to reach the academic unit—is the status of auxiliary services, such as student housing or campus bookstores. The general rule, articulated *In re Atlantic Coast Conference* (1993), is that an auxiliary service is exempt from local taxation if:

* The property at issue is owned by an educational institution;
* The owner is a nonprofit entity;
* The property is used for activities incident to the operation of an educational institution; and

- The property is used only for educational purposes (Kaplin and Lee 1995).

Campus housing used by presidents has been held to be tax exempt, because it is often used for university-related entertaining. The same cannot likely be said of housing for other university employees, such as provosts, business vice presidents, or presidents emeriti, however. Student housing is usually exempt, but courts are mixed on whether fraternities and sororities are exempt, depending upon whether they define Greek houses as educational or social (Kaplin and Lee 1995).

Finally, schools and departments are often the recipients of grants and gifts from outside donors, which take two basic forms: outright gifts of cash, securities, real property, or tangible personal property; and planned gifts contained in wills, various types of trusts, annuities, or life insurance. Academic administrators need to be aware of the difficulties and limits sometimes attendant to the institution's accepting outside grants and gifts. For example, a potentially problematic gift is an endowment for a scholarship restricted to a particular group of students (say, for white males only), with legal and political complications in the context of constitutional law and the antidiscrimination statutes likely. Another example of a possible problem is the donation of real property with an undisclosed but later discovered environmental problem, as environmental laws hold the current owner responsible for problems with toxic or hazardous waste (F. Smith 1993).

Institutions should be especially watchful when accepting outside gifts that are likely to offend limitations imposed by local, state, or federal law, or run counter to limitations imposed by the founding, controlling, or operational documents of the institution, such as its charter or bylaws (F. Smith 1993). Moreover, institutions should develop provisions that limit gifts or grants that would:

- Be too restrictive in purpose or that fail to conform with the institution's academic purposes and priorities;
- Impinge upon the institution's right to accept other gifts or grants;
- Adversely affect the academic freedom of faculty or the rights of students; and
- Subject the institution to adverse publicity (F. Smith 1993).

Deans and chairs should work with institutional development staff in navigating such issues.

Accreditation

Most deans and chairs are involved in an accreditation process during their time on the job. Accreditation is typically
through private associations that act as quasi-regulators of
higher education. An institution can seek two types of accreditation. *Program accreditation* is granted after evaluating
particular schools or departments within an institution and is
often conducted by or in association with professional associations, such as the American Bar Association in law. *Institutional accreditation* applies to the entire institution and is
conducted by one of six regional accrediting agencies, such
as the Middle States Association of Colleges and Schools
(Prairie and Chamberlain 1994).

The essential purposes of accreditation are to ensure and
improve the quality of programs. These ends typically are
accomplished through a two-step process. The program or
institution seeking initial accreditation or reaffirmation of
existing accreditation prepares a comprehensive self-study,
which is reviewed by a team of outside administrators and
educators who visit the campus. The evaluation team then
submits a report and recommendations to the governing
board of the accrediting association, which then makes the
final decision to grant, reaffirm, or deny accreditation. The
program or institution usually has the right to appeal any
adverse decision (Prairie and Chamberlain 1994).

Problems occur when associations deny accreditation.
The traditional judicial deference to decisions in higher education applies in the context of accreditation. One approach
has been to challenge negative assessments under antitrust
law, but these attempts have commonly failed. Antitrust law
is sometimes found to apply to accrediting agencies, but it is
rare that a violation is found. Similarly, the courts rarely find
that constitutional standards, particularly due process, apply
to accrediting agencies. Agencies are not typically held to be
state actors, and thus the decision of the agency is deemed
not to be that of the state but of a private entity to which
constitutional provisions do not apply (Pelesh 1995).

What gives the argument of state action any chance of
succeeding is that the federal government sometimes relies

upon the decisions of accrediting agencies to identify institutions that are eligible for participation in federal programs (Prairie and Chamberlain 1994). In *Parsons College v. North Central Assn. of Colleges and Secondary Schools* (1967) and *Marlboro Corp. v. Assn. of Independent Colleges and Schools* (1977), accrediting agencies were not found to be state actors, but in *Marjorie Webster Junior College v. Middle States Assn. of Colleges and Secondary Schools* (1969), the accrediting agency was held to be a quasi-governmental actor. State action alone does not reverse a negative decision about accreditation; it only gives the institution the right to argue that a constitutionally prohibited deprivation of liberty or property occurred as a result of inadequate notice and hearing provided by the accrediting body. The institution still must prove the alleged deprivation of rights. Finally, defamation can sometimes be an issue in the context of accreditation, but courts will likely not apply standards so strictly that the fear of a successful defamation action will discourage the candid criticism necessary to the success of any accrediting process (Kaplin and Lee 1995).

What does apply to accrediting agencies is the common law (Kaplin and Lee 1995). Accrediting agencies must act fairly and follow their own rules. According to the decision in *Parsons College,* fairness generally involves some amount of procedural due process, however rudimentary. The court in *Marjorie Webster* held that following rules involves reasonableness, evenhandedness, and consistency with public policy. Appropriate measures to ensure procedural due process in accreditation, in addition to compliance with published procedures, should include:

- Freedom from bias or conflict of interest;
- Notice of charges;
- The opportunity to be heard;
- Sufficiently defined standards of accreditation;
- Representation by counsel;
- The right to cross-examine witnesses; and
- The right to appeal (Prairie and Chamberlain 1994).

—oOo—

The intersections between the law and the administration of academic programs and services in higher education are

numerous and significant. Fortunately, a vast research literature is available related to the legal issues that arise when
school deans and department chairs perform their many
duties. With an understanding of the sources of the law, the
roles of counsel, and the judicial process—as well as the
foundations and applications of legal doctrine in higher
education in the areas of employment, student affairs, and
external regulation—academic administrators can successfully navigate legal issues in the school or department.

REFERENCES

The Educational Resources Information Center (ERIC) Clearinghouse on Higher Education abstracts and indexes the current literature on higher education for inclusion in ERIC's database and an-
nouncement in ERIC's monthly bibliographic journal, *Resources in
Education* (RIE). Most of these publications are available through
the ERIC Document Reproduction Service (EDRS). For publications
cited in this bibliography that are available from EDRS, ordering
number and price code are included. Readers who wish to order a
publication should write to the ERIC Document Reproduction Service, 7420 Fullerton Road, Suite 110, Springfield, Virginia 22153-
2852. (Phone orders with VISA or MasterCard are taken at (800)
443-ERIC or (703) 440-1400.) When ordering, please specify the
document (ED) number. Documents are available as noted in mi-
crofiche (MF) and paper copy (PC). If you have the price code
ready when you call, EDRS can quote an exact price. The last page
of the latest issue of *Resources in Education* also has the current
cost, listed by code.

Court Cases
Adarand Constructors, Inc. v. Pena, 515 U.S. 200 (1995).
Basic Books v. Kinko's Graphics Corp., 758 F. Supp. 1522 (S.D.N.Y.
    1991).
Board of Regents v. Roth, 408 U.S. at 573, 92 S. Ct. at 2707 (1972).
Bob Jones University v. United States, 461 U.S. 574 (1983).
Brown v. Board of Education, 374 U.S. 483 (1954).
City of Richmond v. J.A. Crowson Co., 488 U.S. 469 (1989).
Clark v. Community for Creative Non-Violence, 468 U.S. 288
    (1984).
Connick v. Myers, 461 U.S. 138 (1983).
Dixon v. Alabama State Board of Education, 294 F.2d 150 (5th Cir.
    1961).
Gay Rights Coalition of Georgetown University Law Center v.
    Georgetown University, 536 A.2d 1 (D.C. 1987).
Goldfarb v. Virginia State Bar, 421 U.S. 773 (1975).
Griswold v. Connecticut, 381 U.S. 479 (1965).
Harris v. Forklift Systems, 114 S. Ct. 367 (1986).
Healy v. James, 408 U.S. 169 (1972).
Hopwood v. State of Texas, 78 F.3d 932 (5th Cir. 1996).
In re Atlantic Coast Conference, 434 S.E.2d 865 (N.C. Ct. App. 1993).
Johnson v. Transportation Agency, Santa Clara County, 480 U.S. 616
    (1987).
Marjorie Webster Junior College v. Middle States Assn. of Colleges
    and Secondary Schools, 302 F. Supp. 459 (D.D.C. 1969).
Marlboro Corp. v. Assn. of Independent Colleges and Schools, 556
    F.2d 78 (1st Cir. 1977).

Meritor Savings Bank v. Vinson, 477 U.S. 57 (1986).

Mississippi University for Women v. Hogan, 458 U.S. 718 (1982).

National Treasury Employees Union v. Von Raabe, 489 U.S. 656 (1989).

NLRB v. Yeshiva University, 444 U.S. 672 (1980).

Papish v. Board of Curators of the University of Missouri, 410 U.S. 667 (1973).

Parsons College v. North Central Assn. of Colleges and Secondary Schools, 271 F. Supp. 65 (N.D. Ill. 1967).

Perry v. Sindermann, 408 U.S. 593 (1972).

Pickering v. Board of Education, 391 U.S. 563 (1968).

Podberesky v. Kirwan, 764 F. Supp. 364 (D. Md. 1991).

Regents of the University of California v. Bakke, 438 U.S. 265 (1978).

Regents of the University of Michigan v. Ewing, 474 U.S. 214, 226 n. 12 (1985).

Rosenburger v. Rector and Visitors of the University of Virginia, 795 F. Supp. 175 (W.D. Va. 1992), aff'd, 18 F.3d 269 (4th Cir. 1994).

Shamloo v. Mississippi State Board of Trustees, 620 F.2d 516 (5th Cir. 1980).

Skinner v. Railway Labor Executives Association, 489 U.S. 602 (1989).

Southeastern Community College v. Davis, 442 U.S. 397 (1979).

Sweezy v. New Hampshire, 354 U.S. 234 (1957).

United Mine Workers v. Gibbs, 383 U.S. 715 (1966).

University of Pennsylvania v. EEOC, 493 U.S. 182 (1990).

Ward v. Rock Against Racism, 491 U.S. 781 (1989).

Weber v. Kaiser Aluminum Co., 443 U.S. 193 (1979).

Widmar v. Vincent, 454 U.S. 263 (1981).

Worldwide Volkswagen Corp. v. Woodson, 444 U.S. 286 (1980).

Wygant v. Jackson Board of Education, 476 U.S. 267 (1986).

Books and Journals

Adler, Robert S., and Ellen R. Peirce. 1993. "The Legal, Ethical, Social Implications of the 'Reasonable Woman' Standard in Sexual Harassment Cases." *Fordham Law Review* 61: 773–827.

Adler, Sara. 1994. "Arbitration and the Americans with Disabilities Act." *St. Louis University Law Journal* 37: 1005–14.

Allen, Ben T. 1995. *Preventing Sexual Harassment on Campus: Policies and Practices for Higher Education.* Washington, D.C.: College and University Personnel Association. ED 388 159. 67 pp. MF–01; PC not available EDRS.

American Association of Collegiate Registrars and Admissions Officers. 1989. "Misrepresentation in the Marketplace: Recognizing Fraudulent Credentials." In *College and Student Records: A Legal Compendium,* edited by Joan E. Van Tol. Washington, D.C.: National Association of College and University Attorneys.

American Association of University Professors. May/June 1992. "College and University Policies on Substance Abuse and Drug Testing." *Academe:* 17–23.

Araujo, Robert John. 1996. "'The Harvest Is Plentiful, but the Laborers are Few': Hiring Practices and Religiously Affiliated Universities." *University of Richmond Law Review* 30: 713–80.

Association of American Medical Colleges. 1993. "The Americans with Disabilities Act (ADA) and the Disabled Student in Medical School." In *Accommodating Students with Learning and Emotional Disabilities: A Legal Compendium,* edited by Richard B. Crockett and Shelley Sanders Kehl (1996). Washington, D.C.: National Association of College and University Attorneys.

Association of the Bar of the City of New York, Special Committee on Education and the Law. 1989. "Due Process in Decisions Related to Tenure in Higher Education." *Journal of College and University Law* 11(3): 323–44.

Baida, Andrew H. 1992. "Not All Minority Scholarships Are Created Equal: Why Some May Be More Constitutional Than Others." *Journal of College and University Law* 18(3): 333–66.

———. 1994. "Not All Minority Scholarships Are Created Equal. Part 2: How to Develop a Record That Passes Constitutional Scrutiny." *Journal of College and University Law* 21(2): 307–52.

Barnes, Thomas J., and David E. Khorey. 1989. "The Effects and Use of Administrative Determinations in Subsequent Employment Litigation." *Journal of College and University Law* 16(2): 189–200.

Barr, Margaret J. 1996. "Legal Foundations of Student Affairs Practice." In *Student Services: A Handbook for the Profession,* edited by Susan R. Komives, Dudley B. Woodard, Jr., and Associates. San Francisco: Jossey-Bass.

Bazluke, Francine Tilewick. 1996. *Defamation Issues in Higher Education.* 2d ed. Washington, D.C.: National Association of College and University Attorneys.

Bednash, Geraldine (Polly). 1991. "Tenure Review: Process and Outcomes." *Review of Higher Education* 15(1): 47–63.

Belch, Holley A. 1994. "Professionals with Disabilities." In *A Student Affairs Guide to the ADA and Disability Issues,* edited by Dan Ryan and Maureen McCarthy. Washington, D.C.: National Association of Student Personnel Administrators.

Bell, Edwin D. 1991. "Affirmative Action in Postsecondary Education: The Education of Civilized Primates." *College Student Journal* 25: 331–35.

Benedict, Forest C., and Cynthia Smith. 1992. "Supervisor's Guide to Effective Performance Appraisal." Washington, D.C.: College and University Personnel Association.

Bennett, Barbara. 1990. "Risky Business: Risk Management, Loss Prevention, and Insurance Procurement for Colleges and Universities." Washington, D.C.: National Association of College and University Attorneys. ED 410 838. 30 pp. MF–01; PC not available EDRS.

Bernard, Pamela J. 1989. "Liability Releases in the University Setting." In *Am I Liable? Faculty, Staff, and Institutional Liability in the College and University Setting.* Washington, D.C.: National Association of College and University Attorneys.

Bernhardt, Herbert N. 1993. "Affirmative Action in Employment: Considering Group Interests While Protecting Individual Rights." *Stetson Law Review* 23: 11–37.

Bickel, Robert D. 1994. "A Revisitation of the Role of College and University Legal Counsel." *West's Education Law Quarterly* 3(11): 161–70.

Bickel, Robert D., and Peter F. Lake. 1994. "Reconceptualizing the University's Duty to Provide a Safe Learning Environment: A Criticism of the Doctrine of In Loco Parentis and the Restatement (Second) of Torts." *Journal of College and University Law* 20(3): 261–94.

Birnbaum, David N. 1995. "Violence in the Workplace." In *Employment Issues in Higher Education: A Legal Compendium,* edited by Jean S. Sagan and Thomas P. Rebel. Washington, D.C.: National Association of College and University Attorneys. ED 378 932. 532 pp. MF–02; PC not available EDRS.

Bonham, V.L. 1989. "Academic Advising and Defamation in the Context of Academic Evaluation." In *Am I Liable? Faculty, Staff, and Institutional Liability in the College and University Setting.* Washington, D.C.: National Association of College and University Attorneys.

Boston University Faculty Council on Academic Freedom. 1996. "Report of the Boston University Faculty Council on Academic Freedom." Boston: Boston Univ.

Bracewell, William R. 1978. "An Application of the Privacy Concept to Student Life." In *The Legal Foundations of Student Personnel Services in Higher Education,* edited by Edward Hammond and Robert Shaffer. Washington, D.C.: American College Personnel Association.

Bremer, Barbara A., Cathleen T. Moore, and Ellen F. Bildersee. 1991. "Do You Have to Call It 'Sexual Harassment' to Feel Harassed?" *College Student Journal* 25: 258–68.

Brinckerhoff, Loring C., and Joan M. McGuire. 1994. "Students with Learning Disabilities: Programmatic and Instructional Considerations." In *A Student Affairs Guide to the ADA and Disability Issues,* edited by Dan Ryan and Maureen McCarthy. Washington, D.C.: National Association of Student Personnel Administrators.

Broadhurst, Arthur G. 1996. "Is Sovereign Immunity Archaic? Protections for Colleges and Universities Continue to Erode." *Busi-*

ness Officer 29(1): 40–43.

Brockmeyer, M., and G. Fowler. 1982. "The Law and Professional School Admissions." *College and University* 57(2): 117–34.

Brooks, Brian G. 1995. "Adequate Cause for Dismissal: The Missing Element in Academic Freedom." *Journal of College and University Law* 22(2): 331–58.

Brooks, Timothy F. 1994. "A Gathering Storm. Legal Issues Concerning Students with Disabilities: An Analysis of OCR Interpretations." In *Accommodating Students with Learning and Emotional Disabilities: A Legal Compendium,* edited by Richard B. Crockett and Shelley Sanders Kehl (1996). Washington, D.C.: National Association of College and University Attorneys.

Brown, J. Noah. 1996. "Spotlight on Working Adults: Congress Threatens Tax Exemption of Employer-Provided Tuition Assistance." *Educational Record* 77(1): 18–19.

Brown, Jane T. 1994. "Effective Disability Support Services Programs." In *A Student Affairs Guide to the ADA and Disability Issues,* edited by Dan Ryan and Maureen McCarthy. Washington, D.C.: National Association of Student Personnel Administrators.

Brown, Kathryn A. 1996. "ADA: Disorders of the Mind." In *Accommodating Students with Learning and Emotional Disabilities: A Legal Compendium,* edited by Richard B. Crockett and Shelley Sanders Kehl. Washington, D.C.: National Association of College and University Attorneys.

Brown, Sharon E., and Kim Cannon. 1993. "Educational Malpractice Actions: A Remedy for What Ails Our Schools?" *Education Law Quarterly* 2(2): 246–57.

Brown, Valerie L. 1990. "A Comparative Analysis of College Autonomy in Selected States." *Education Law Reporter* 60(2): 299–312.

Bunting, Elizabeth. 1990. "The Admissions Process: New Legal Questions Creep Up the Ivory Tower." *West's Education Law Reporter* 60(3): 691–97.

Burg, Halee. 1995. "Memorandum Re: Post-Tenure Faculty Evaluation." In *Employment Issues in Higher Education: A Legal Compendium,* edited by Jean S. Sagan and Thomas P. Rebel. Washington, D.C.: National Association of College and University Attorneys. ED 378 932. 532 pp. MF–02; PC not available EDRS.

Burgoyne, Robert A. 1992. "The Copyright Remedy Clarification Act of 1990: State Educational Institutions Now Face Significant Monetary Exposure for Copyright Infringement." *Journal of College and University Law* 18(3): 367–80.

Burgoyne, Robert A., and Jacqueline R. Depew. 1993. "The Americans with Disabilities Act." In *Accommodating Students with Learning and Emotional Disabilities: A Legal Compendium,* edited by Richard B. Crockett and Shelley Sanders Kehl (1996). Washington, D.C.: National Association of College and University Attorneys.

Burke, William T., and Frank J. Cavaliere. 1991. "Equal Employment Opportunity on Campus: Strengthening the Commitment." *Labor Law Journal* 42: 19–27.

Burling, Phillip. 1991. "Crime on Campus: Analyzing and Managing the Increasing Risk of Institutional Liability." Washington, D.C.: National Association of College and University Attorneys. ED 374 764. 43 pp. MF–01; PC not available EDRS.

Burling, Phillip, and Katherine A. Matthews. 1992. "Responding to Whistleblowers: An Analysis of Whistleblower Protection Acts and the Practical Consequences." Washington, D.C.: National Association of College and University Attorneys. ED 349 916. 33 pp. MF–01; PC not available EDRS.

Burnett, Collins W., and W.L. Matthews. 1982. "The Legalistic Culture in American Higher Education." *College and University* 57(2): 197–207.

Butner, Blain B., and David B. Rigney. 1993. "Managing Federal Student Financial Aid Programs." Washington, D.C.: National Association of College and University Attorneys. ED 363 182. 30 pp. MF–01; PC not available EDRS.

Capano, Kathleen M. 1991. "Stopping Students from Cheating: Halting the Activities of Term Paper Mills and Enforcing Disciplinary Sanctions against Students who Purchase Term Papers." *Journal of College and University Law* 18(2): 277–98.

Carkeek, Susan, et al. 1988. "A Practical Guide to the Employment Function." Washington, D.C.: College and University Personnel Association.

Carroll, Constance M. 1993. "Sexual Harassment on Campus: Enhancing Awareness and Promoting Change." *Educational Record* 74(1): 21–26.

Cherry, Robert L., Jr., and John P. Geary. 1992. "The College Catalog as a Contract." *Journal of Law and Education* 21(1): 1–32.

Ciesla, A.M. June 1994. "Understanding and Preventing Sexual Harassment after *Harris.*" *Practical Lawyer* 40: 15–24.

Cleveland, Harlan. 1985. "The Costs and Benefits of Openness: Sunshine Laws and Higher Education." *Journal of College and University Law* 12(2): 127–73.

———. September/October 1987. "The Costs and Benefits of Openness." *Academe:* 23–28.

Cloud, Robert C. 1992. "The President and the Law." *Educational Record* 73: 7–15.

Cole, Bettie S. 1991. "Legal Issues Related to Social Work Program Admissions." *Journal of Social Work Education* 27(1): 18–24.

Cole, Bettie S., and Robert G. Lewis. 1993. "Gatekeeping through Termination of Unsuitable Social Work Students: Legal Issues and Guidelines." *Journal of Social Work Education* 29(2): 150–59.

Cole, Elsa Kircher. 1994. "Selected Legal Issues Relating to Due Process and Liability in Higher Education." Washington, D.C.: Council of Graduate Schools. ED 370 478. 45 pp. MF–01; PC–02.

———, ed. 1990. *Sexual Harassment on Campus: A Legal Compendium.* Washington, D.C.: National Association of College and University Attorneys.

Cole, Elsa Kircher, and B.L. Shiels, eds. 1989. *Student Legal Issues.* Washington, D.C.: National Association of College and University Attorneys.

Connolly, Walter B., and Alison B. Marshall. 1989. "Sexual Harassment of University or College Students by Faculty Members." *Journal of College and University Law* 15(4): 381–403.

Cooper, Diane L., and James M. Lancaster. 1995. "The Legal and Developmental Perspectives: A Question of Balance." *College Student Affairs Journal* 14(1): 5–15.

Copeland, John D., and John W. Murry, Jr. 1996. "Getting Tossed from the Ivory Tower: The Legal Implications of Evaluating Faculty Performance." *Missouri Law Review* 61(2): 238–327.

Craver, Charles B. 1990. "The Implications of the Elimination of Mandatory Retirement for Professors." *Journal of College and University Law* 16(3): 343–72.

Crenshaw, Carrie. 1995. "The 'Protection' of 'Women': A History of Legal Attitudes toward Women's Workplace Freedom." *Quarterly Journal of Speech* 81(1): 63–82.

Crews, Kenneth D. 1993. *Copyright, Fair Use, and the Challenge for Universities.* Chicago: Univ. of Chicago Press.

———. 1995. "Copyright Law and Information Policy Planning: Public Rights of Use in the 1990s and Beyond." *Journal of Government Information* 22(2): 87–99.

Crockett, Richard B. 5 November 1992. "Accommodation of Students with Disabilities." In *Accommodating Students with Learning and Emotional Disabilities: A Legal Compendium,* edited by Richard B. Crockett and Shelley Sanders Kehl (1996). Washington, D.C.: National Association of College and University Attorneys.

———. 8 March 1994. "Auxiliary Aids and Services for Hearing-impaired Students." In *Accommodating Students with Learning and Emotional Disabilities: A Legal Compendium,* edited by Richard B. Crockett and Shelley Sanders Kehl (1996). Washington, D.C.: National Association of College and University Attorneys.

Crockett, Richard B., and Shelley Sanders Kehl. 1996. "Introduction." In *Accommodating Students with Learning and Emotional Disabilities: A Legal Compendium,* edited by Richard B. Crockett and Shelley Sanders Kehl. Washington, D.C.: National Association of College and University Attorneys.

Daane, Roderick. 1985. "The Role of University Counsel." *Journal of College and University Law* 12(3): 399–414.

Davenport, David. 1985. "The Catalog in the Classroom: From

Shield to Sword." *Journal of College and University Law* 12(2): 201–26.

Davis, Charles N. 1994. "Libel and Statements of Opinion before and after *Milkovich.*" *Newspaper Research Journal* 15(3): 105–21.

Deasy, Robert P. 1994. "Immigration Options for Professors and Researchers." Washington, D.C.: American Immigration Lawyers Association.

DiGiovanni, Nicholas, Jr. 1989. "Age Discrimination: An Administrator's Guide." Washington, D.C.: College and University Personnel Association.

DiGiovanni, Nicholas. 1993a. "The Legal Aspects of the Aging Work Force." In *The Aging Work Force: A Guide for Higher Education Administrators,* edited by Nancy B. Julius and Herbert H. Krauss. Washington, D.C.: College and University Personnel Association.

———. 1993b. "The Preparation of Labor Arbitration Cases." In *Managing the Industrial Labor Relations Process in Higher Education,* edited by Daniel J. Julius. Washington, D.C.: College and University Personnel Association.

DiScala, Jeanette, Steven G. Olswang, and Carol S. Niccolls. 1992. "College and University Responses to the Emotionally or Mentally Impaired Student." *Journal of College and University Law* 19(1): 17–34.

Dixon, Thomas M., Daniel F. Lynch, and Lisa L. Swem. 1987. "Case Comment. *Pace v. Hymans*—Termination of Tenured University Faculty: Financial Exigency and the Burden of Proof in a Substantive Due Process Claim." *Journal of College and University Law* 13(4): 417–28.

Doughtrey, William H., Jr. 1991. "The Legal Nature of Academic Freedom in United States Colleges and Universities." *University of Richmond Law Review* 25(1): 233–71.

Douvanis, Costas J., and John A. Brown. 1993. "Confidential and Privileged Communications: Legal and Ethical Concepts in Research." *Mid-Western Educational Researcher* 6(1): 2–6.

Drapeau, Donald A. 1995. "Tenure Traps: Legal Issues of Concern." *Journal of the Association for Communication* 1: 60–63.

Drimmer, Jonathan C. 1993. "Cripples, Overcomers, and Civil Rights: Tracing the Evolution of Federal Legislation and Social Policy for People with Disabilities." *UCLA Law Review* 40: 1341–1410.

Drinan, Robert F. 1993. "Lawyer-Client Confidentiality in the Campus Setting." *Journal of College and University Law* 19(4): 305–14.

Duchin, Robert. 1991. "Christian and Secular Workplaces Contrasted." In *Human Resource Management in Religiously Affiliated Institutions,* edited by Barbara Nicholson-Brown. Washington, D.C.: College and University Personnel Association.

Duffy, Dennis P. 1995. "Personnel Policies and Employee Handbooks." In *Employment Issues in Higher Education: A Legal Com-*

pendium, edited by Jean S. Sagan and Thomas P. Rebel. Washington, D.C.: National Association of College and University Attorneys. ED 378 932. 532 pp. MF–02; PC not available EDRS.

Duffy, J. Trey. 1994. "Psychological Disabilities." In *A Student Affairs Guide to the ADA and Disability Issues,* edited by Dan Ryan and Maureen McCarthy. Washington, D.C.: National Association of Student Personnel Administrators.

Dunham, Stephen S. 1993. "Case Studies on Wrongdoing on Campus: Ethics and the Lawyer's Role." *Journal of College and University Law* 19(4): 315–32.

Duston, Robert L., Karen S. Russell, and Lynn E. Kerr. 1992. "A Guide to Writing Job Descriptions under the Americans with Disabilities Act." Washington, D.C.: College and University Personnel Association.

———. 1993. "Hiring: Dos and Don'ts for Interviewing under the ADA." Washington, D.C.: College and University Personnel Association.

Eames, Patricia, and Thomas P. Hustoles, eds. 1989. *Legal Issues in Faculty Employment.* Washington, D.C.: National Association of College and University Attorneys.

Edwards, Harry T., and Virginia Davis Nordin. 1979. *Higher Education and the Law.* Cambridge, Mass.: Harvard Univ. Press.

———. 1981. *Higher Education and the Law: 1981 Cumulative Supplement.* Cambridge, Mass.: Harvard Univ. Press.

Edwards, Margaret H. 1992–93. "The ADA and Employment of Individuals with Mental Disabilities." *Employee Relations Law Journal* 18(3): 347–89.

Edwards, Robert W. 1994. "The Rights of Students with Learning Disabilities and the Responsibilities of Institutions of Higher Education under the Americans with Disabilities Act." *Journal of Law and Policy* 2: 213–48.

Elza, Jane. 1993. "Liability and Penalties for Sexual Harassment in Higher Education." *Education Law Reporter* 78: 235–45.

Estey, Martin. May/June 1986. "Faculty Grievance Procedures outside Collective Bargaining: The Experience of AAU Campuses." *Academe:* 6–15.

Fay, John F. 1993. "An Introduction to Arbitration." *Utah Bar Journal* 6(2): 16–18.

Fellrath, Abbie F. 1996. "*Coleman v. Zatechka:* The ADA and Student Life." *Journal of College and University Law* 23(2): 285–300.

Finaldi, Anthony K. 1995. "The *Vaksman* Approach to Academic Dismissals: A Different Beat to the Same Drum." *Journal of Law and Education* 24(3): 499–503.

Finkin, Matthew W. 1988. "Tenure after an Uncapped ADEA: A Different View." *Journal of College and University Law* 15(1): 43–60.

Finnie, Bob, and Gloria Finnie. 1993. "Good Endings: Managing

Employee Terminations." Washington, D.C.: College and University Personnel Association. ED 000 230. 26 pp. MF–01; PC not available EDRS.

Fishbein, Estelle A. 1991. "Ownership of Research Data." *Academic Medicine* 66(3): 129–33.

Floerchinger, Debra. 1995. "The Diet Cola Man and Other Fantasies: Sexual Assertiveness or Harassment?" *Campus Activities Programming* 28(1): 22–26.

Flygare, Thomas J. 1995. "The Family and Medical Leave Act of 1993: Applications in Higher Education." Washington, D.C.: National Association of College and University Attorneys. ED 374 763. 17 pp. MF–01; PC not available EDRS.

Ford, Robert L. 1993. *Interview Guide for Supervisors.* 4th ed. Washington, D.C.: College and University Personnel Association.

Fortunato, Ray T., and James M. Elliott. 1992. *A Handbook for Developing Higher Education Personnel Policies.* Washington, D.C.: College and University Personnel Association.

Franke, Ann H., and Jacqueline W. Mintz. September/October 1987. "Four Trends in Higher Education Law." *Academe:* 57–63.

Fried, Barbara. 1994. "Domestic Partner Benefits: A Case Study." Washington, D.C.: College and University Personnel Association.

Garfield, Lesley Yalof. 1996. "Squaring Affirmative Action Admissions Policies with Federal Judicial Guidelines: A Model for the Twenty-first Century." *Journal of College and University Law* 22(4): 895–934.

Gehring, Donald D., Kenneth J. Osfield, and Judy Wald. 1994. "Legal, Ethical, and Policy Implications of the Americans with Disabilities Act." In *A Student Affairs Guide to the ADA and Disability Issues,* edited by Dan Ryan and Maureen McCarthy. Washington, D.C.: National Association of Student Personnel Administrators.

Gerry, Frank C. 1993. "Faculty Workload and Productivity." In *Managing the Industrial Labor Relations Process in Higher Education,* edited by Daniel J. Julius. Washington, D.C.: College and University Personnel Association.

Gibbs, Annette. 1995. "Student Activity Fees and the Courts: Rights of Speech and Association." *NASPA Journal* 32(3): 232–38.

Gibbs, Annette, and Don Gehring. 1996. "What the Supreme Court Said in *Rosenburger:* Who Knows?" *Journal of College Student Development* 37(1): 3–6.

Gillepsie, Patti P. 1985. "Department Chairs and the Law." *ACA Bulletin* 51: 22–25.

Gordon, Joan I. 1991. "Issues Related to Disabled Students and Implementation of the Americans with Disabilities Act." In *Accommodating Students with Learning and Emotional Disabilities: A Legal Compendium,* edited by Richard B. Crockett and Shelley Sanders Kehl (1996). Washington, D.C.: National Association of

College and University Attorneys.

Greenleaf, Cynthia. 1985. "Academic Institutions in the Light and Shadow of the Law." *Journal of College and University Law* 12(1): 1–40.

Greenleaf, E.A. 1978. "The Relationship of Legal Issues and Procedures to Student Development." In *Legal Foundations of Student Personnel Services in Higher Education,* edited by Edward Hammond and Robert Shaffer. Washington, D.C.: American College Personnel Association.

Gregory, Dennis E. 1991. "The Role of College and University Legal Counsel with Regard to Operational or Policy-Making Responsibilities for Student Issues on Campus." *College Student Affairs Journal* 10(3): 26–40.

Grexa, Thomas. 1992. "Title VII Tenure Litigation in the Academy and Academic Freedom: A Current Appraisal." *Dickinson Law Review* 96: 11–36.

Grey, Thomas C. 1992. "Civil Rights vs. Civil Liberties." *Journal of Higher Education* 63: 485–516.

Gulland, Eugene D. 1989. "Selected Issues Involving Student Groups and Alcohol-Related Liability." In *Am I Liable? Faculty, Staff, and Institutional Liability in the College and University Setting.* Washington, D.C.: National Association of College and University Attorneys.

———. 1994. "Developing Effective and Legally Sound Alcohol Policies: How Well Does Your Alcohol Policy Work?" Washington, D.C.: National Association of Student Personnel Administrators.

Gunter, T. Luther, and Joseph Orndorff. 1989. "Transcript Seals: Let's Take Another Look." In *College and Student Records: A Legal Compendium,* edited by Joan E. Van Tol. Washington, D.C.: National Association of College and University Attorneys.

Hagen, Janet W., and Willis W. Hagen. 1995. "What Employment Counselors Need to Know about Employment Discrimination and the Civil Rights Act." *Journal of Employment Counseling* 32(1): 2–10.

Haggard, Loretta K. 1993. "Reasonable Accommodations of Individuals with Mental Disabilities and Psychoactive Substance Use Disorders under Title I of the Americans with Disabilities Act." *Journal of Urban and Contemporary Law* 43: 343–90.

Hammond, Edward H. 1978. "The Consumer-Institutional Relationship." In *The Legal Foundations of Student Personnel Services in Higher Education,* edited by Edward Hammond and Robert Shaffer. Washington, D.C.: American College Personnel Association.

Harper, Michael C. 1993. "Age-Based Exit Incentives, Coercion, and the Prospective Waiver of ADEA Rights: The Failure of the Older Workers Benefit Protection Act." *Virginia Law Review* 79(6):

1271–1344.

Harris, Richard R., Christy A. Horn, and Maureen A. McCarthy. 1994. "Physical and Technological Access." In *A Student Affairs Guide to the ADA and Disability Issues,* edited by Dan Ryan and Maureen McCarthy. Washington, D.C.: National Association of Student Personnel Administrators.

Heffernan, Elizabeth B., and Francine T. Bazluke. 1996. "Minority-Targeted Admissions and Financial Aid Programs." Washington, D.C.: National Association of College and University Attorneys.

Heinemann, Lynne E. 1995. "Employees with Infectious Diseases: Testing and Accommodation." In *Employment Issues in Higher Education: A Legal Compendium,* edited by Jean S. Sagan and Thomas P. Rebel. Washington, D.C.: National Association of College and University Attorneys.

Hemnes, Thomas M.S., Alexander H. Pyle, and Laurie M. McTeague. 1994. "A Guide to Copyright Issues." Washington, D.C.: National Association of College and University Attorneys. ED 374 762. 17 pp. MF–01; PC not available EDRS.

Hendrickson, Robert. 1990. "Legal Issues Surrounding the Tenure Decision in Higher Education." *West's Education Law Reporter* 58(2): 433–43.

———. 1996 (editions back to 1972). "Higher Education." In *Yearbook of Education Law, 1996,* edited by Charles J. Russo. Dayton: Education Law Association.

Hendrickson, Robert M., and Annette Gibbs. 1986. *The College, the Constitution, and the Consumer Student: Implications for Policy and Practice.* ASHE-ERIC Higher Education Report No. 7. Washington, D.C.: Association for the Study of Higher Education. ED 280 429. 108 pp. MF–01; PC–05.

Hernandez, Wendy. 1994. "The Constitutionality of Racially Restrictive Organizations within the University Setting." *Journal of College and University Law* 21(2): 429–53.

Hiers, Richard H. 1995. "New Restrictions on Academic Free Speech: *Jeffries v. Harleston II." Journal of College and University Law* 22(2): 217–80.

Hirschfeld, Stephen J. 1995. "Employee Misconduct—On and Off Duty." In *Employment Issues in Higher Education: A Legal Compendium,* edited by Jean S. Sagan and Thomas P. Rebel. Washington, D.C.: National Association of College and University Attorneys. ED 378 932. 532 pp. MF–02; PC not available EDRS.

Horan, Margaret Healy. 1991. "Faculty Compensation at Religiously Affiliated Institutions." In *Human Resource Management in Religiously Affiliated Institutions,* edited by Barbara Nicholson-Brown. Washington, D.C.: College and University Personnel Association.

Houpt, Corinne A. 1992. "Handling Employees in Downsizing." In

Employment Issues in Higher Education: A Legal Compendium,
edited by Jean S. Sagan and Thomas P. Rebel. Washington, D.C.:
National Association of College and University Attorneys. ED
378 932. 532 pp. MF–02; PC not available EDRS.

Hurd, Richard W. 1993. "The Unionization of Clerical, Technical, and
Professional Employees in Higher Education." In *Managing the
Industrial Labor Relations Process in Higher Education,* edited by
Daniel J. Julius. Washington, D.C.: College and University Per-
sonnel Association.

Hustoles, Thomas P. 1995. "Dealing with Employee Misconduct
(On and Off Duty)." In *Employment Issues in Higher Education:
A Legal Compendium,* edited by Jean S. Sagan and Thomas P.
Rebel. Washington, D.C.: National Association of College and
University Attorneys. ED 378 932. 532 pp. MF–02; PC not avail-
able EDRS.

Hustoles, Thomas P., and Charles A. Doerr. 1983–84. "Faculty and
Staff Dismissals: Developing Contract and Tort Theories." *Journal of College and University Law* 10(4): 479–94.

Hyman, Ursula H. 1989. "The Family Educational Rights and Privacy Act of 1974 and College Records Systems of the Future." In
College and Student Records: A Legal Compendium, edited by
Joan E. Van Tol. Washington, D.C.: National Association of College and University Attorneys.

Jackson, Brian. 1991. "The Lingering Legacy of In Loco Parentis: A
Historical Survey and Proposal for Reform." *Vanderbilt Law Review* 44: 1135–64.

James, Ronald J., Angel Gomez, and Brian W. Bulgar. 1995. "Current Legal Trends in Employee Selection Procedures." In *Employment Issues in Higher Education: A Legal Compendium,*
edited by Jean S. Sagan and Thomas P. Rebel. Washington, D.C.:
National Association of College and University Attorneys. ED
378 932. 532 pp. MF–02; PC not available EDRS.

Janosik, Steven M. 1991. "Respondeat Superior: Holding Institutions
Liable for the Torts of Students and Student Organizations."
NASPA Journal 91(28): 263–70.

Jennings, Eileen K. 1981. "Breach of Contract Suits by Students
against Postsecondary Institutions: Can They Succeed?" *Journal
of College and University Law* 7(3): 191–221.

Johnson, Kathryn A. 1993. "Constructive Discharge and 'Reasonable
Discharge' under the Americans with Disabilities Act." *University
of Colorado Law Review* 65: 175–91.

Julian, Frank H. 1995. "The Promise and Perils of the Eleventh
Amendment Immunity in Suits against Public Colleges and
Universities." *South Texas Law Review* 36: 85–108.

Julius, Daniel J. 1991. "Management Practices at Church-Related
Colleges and Universities: Historical and Contemporary Per-

spectives." In *Human Resource Management in Religiously Affiliated Institutions,* edited by Barbara Nicholson-Brown. Washington, D.C.: College and University Personnel Association.

———. 1993a. "Effective Contract Administration." In *Managing the Industrial Labor Relations Process in Higher Education,* edited by Daniel J. Julius. Washington, D.C.: College and University Personnel Association.

———. 1993b. "Introduction. The Status of Employee Unions in Colleges and Universities: 1930s–1990s." In *Managing the Industrial Labor Relations Process in Higher Education,* edited by Daniel J. Julius. Washington, D.C.: College and University Personnel Association.

Kaplin, William A. 1992. "A Proposed Process for Managing the First Amendment Aspects of Campus Hate Speech." *Journal of Higher Education* 63(5): 517–38.

Kaplin, William A., and Barbara A. Lee. 1995. *The Law of Higher Education.* San Francisco: Jossey-Bass.

Kasunic, Robert. 1993. "Fair Use and the Educator's Right to Photocopy Copyrighted Material for Classroom Use." *Journal of College and University Law* 19(3): 271–94.

Kaufman, Hattie E. 1994. *Access to Institutions of Higher Education for Students with Disabilities.* 3d ed. Washington, D.C.: National Association of College and University Attorneys.

Kehl, Shelley Sanders. 1995. "Accommodating Learning-Disabled College Students: Standards of Judicial Review." In *Accommodating Students with Learning and Emotional Disabilities: A Legal Compendium,* edited by Richard B. Crockett and Shelley Sanders Kehl (1996). Washington, D.C.: National Association of College and University Attorneys.

Keller, Elisabeth A. 1988. "Consensual Amorous Relationships between Faculty and Students." *Journal of College and University Law* 15(1): 21–42.

Ketchum, Michele Morgan. 1993. "Academic Decision Making: Law Schools' Discretion under the Americans with Disabilities Act." *UMKC Law Review* 62(1): 209–25.

Klein, Stephen P. 1994. "Are We Leveling or Tilting the Playing Field?" In *Accommodating Students with Learning and Emotional Disabilities: A Legal Compendium,* edited by Richard B. Crockett and Shelley Sanders Kehl (1996). Washington, D.C.: National Association of College and University Attorneys.

Kramer, Karen M. 1995. "The Free Rider Problem and First Amendment Concerns: A Balance Upset by New Limitations on Mandatory Student Fees." *Journal of College and University Law* 21(4): 691–722.

Kruft, Corinne D. 1996. *"McDaniels v. Flick:* Terminating the Employment of Tenured Professors—What Process Is Due?"

Villanova Law Review 41: 607–47.

Kuh, George, James Lyons, Thomas Miller, and Jo Anne Trow. 1994. *Reasonable Expectations: Renewing the Educational Compact between Institutions and Students.* Washington, D.C.: National Association of Student Personnel Administrators.

Laarman, Linda M. 1993. "Employee Health Coverage for Domestic Partners: Identifying the Issues." *Employee Relations Law Journal* 18(4): 567–80.

Lallo, Dina. 1992. "Student Challenges to Grades and Academic Dismissals: Are They Losing Battles?" *Journal of College and University Law* 18(4): 577–94.

LaNoue, George R., and Barbara A. Lee. January/February 1987. "Lawsuits in Academe: Nobody Wins." *AGB Reports* 29(1): 38–42.

Larson, David Allen. 1992. "What You Can Say, Where You Can Say It, and to Whom: A Guide to Understanding and Preventing Sexual Harassment." *Creighton Law Review* 25: 827–54.

Laycock, Douglas. 1993. "The Rights of Religious Academic Communities." *Journal of College and University Law* 20(1): 15–42.

Leap, Terry L. 1995. *Tenure, Discrimination, and the Courts.* 2d ed. Ithaca, N.Y.: Cornell Univ. Press.

Leas, Terence. 1991. "Higher Education, the Courts, and the 'Doctrine' of Academic Abstention." *Journal of Law and Education* 20(2): 135–65.

Lee, Barbara A. 1990. "Peer Review Confidentiality: Is It Still Possible?" Washington, D.C.: National Association of College and University Attorneys. ED 341 336. 25 pp. MF–01; PC not available EDRS.

———. 1993. "Managing Faculty Employment Decisions: Making the System Accountable." In *Managing the Industrial Labor Relations Process in Higher Education,* edited by Daniel J. Julius. Washington, D.C.: College and University Personnel Association.

Lee, Barbara, and James P. Begin. 1983–84. "Criteria for Evaluating the Managerial Status of College Faculty: Applications of *Yeshiva University* by the NLRB." *Journal of College and University Law* 10(4): 515–39.

Lee, Barbara A., and Peter Ruger. 1997. *Accommodating Faculty and Staff with Psychiatric Disabilities.* Washington, D.C.: National Association of College and University Attorneys.

Leland, Dorothy. 1994. "Hurrah for the Reasonable Woman." *Initiatives* 56(3): 1–7.

Leslie, David W. 1986. "Academic Freedom for Universities." *Review of Higher Education* 9(2): 135–57.

Levitov, Peter S. 1992. "Legal Issues Affecting International Students." In *Working with International Students and Scholars on American Campuses,* edited by David McIntire and Patricia Willer. Washington, D.C.: National Association of Student Per-

sonnel Administrators. ED 360 599. 193 pp. MF–01; PC–08.

Lewis, Tammy L., and Lisa A. Vincler. 1994. "Storming the Ivory Tower: The Competing Interests of the Public's Right to Know and Protecting the Integrity of University Research." *Journal of College and University Law* 20(4): 417–60.

Liddell, Debora L., and Costas J. Douvanis. Winter 1994. "The Social and Legal Status of Gay and Lesbian Students: An Update for Colleges and Universities." *NASPA Journal* 31: 121–29.

Liethen, Michael A. 1989. "Falsification of Applications." In *College and Student Records: A Legal Compendium,* edited by Joan E. Van Tol. Washington, D.C.: National Association of College and University Attorneys.

Long, Nicholas Trott. 1985. "Standard of Proof in Student Discipline Cases." *Journal of College and University Law* 12(1): 71–81.

Loren, Frances. 1992. "New Rules for Old Age." In *Employment Issues in Higher Education: A Legal Compendium,* edited by Jean S. Sagan and Thomas P. Rebel. Washington, D.C.: National Association of College and University Attorneys. ED 378 932. 532 pp. MF–02; PC not available EDRS.

Lovely, Linda. 1991. "Beyond the Freedom to Do Good and Not to Teach Evil: Professors' Academic Freedom Rights in Classrooms of Public Higher Education." *Wake Forest Law Review* 26: 711–40.

Lumsden, Linda. 1992. "Sticks and Stones: Why First Amendment Absolutism Fails When Applied to Campus Harassment Codes." Paper presented at an annual meeting of the Association for Education in Journalism and Mass Communication, Montreal, Quebec. ED 351 715. 29 pp. MF–01; PC–02.

Luna, Gaye. 1990. "Understanding Gender-Based Wage Discrimination: Legal Interpretation and Trends of Pay Equity in Higher Education." *Journal of Law Education* 19(3): 371–84.

Lutzker, Arnold P., and Cary A. Eure. December 1993/January 1994. "Technology and Intellectual Property." *AACC Journal:* 24–29.

McCarthy, Martha M. 1985. "Legal Challenges to Academic Decisions in Higher Education." *College and University* 60(2): 99–113.

McCusker, Claire E. 1995. "The Americans with Disabilities Act: Its Potential for Expanding the Scope of Reasonable Academic Accommodations." *Journal of College and University Law* 21(4): 619–42.

McDaniel, Diane L., and Paul Tanaka. 1995. "The Permissibility of Withholding Transcripts under Bankruptcy Law." 2d ed. Washington, D.C.: National Association of College and University Attorneys. ED 394 483. 13 pp. MF–01; PC not available EDRS.

McEvoy, Sharlene A. 1992. "Campus Insecurity: Duty, Foreseeability, and Third Party Liability." *Journal of Law Education* 21(2): 137–54.

McGee, Robert W. 1993. "Academic Tenure: Should It Be Protected by Law?" *Western State Law University Law Review* 20: 593–602.

McHugh, William F. 1973. "Faculty Unionism and Tenure." *Journal of College and University Law* 1(1): 46–74.

McIntire, David, and Patricia Willer, eds. 1992. *Working with International Students and Scholars on American Campuses.* Washington, D.C.: National Association of Student Personnel Administrators. ED 360 599. 193 pp. MF–01; PC–08.

McKee, Patrick W. 1980. "Tenure by Default: The Non-Formal Acquisition of Academic Tenure." *Journal of College and University Law* 7(1–2): 31–56.

McKenna and Cuneo Law Firm. 1995a. "Wrongful Discharge and Other Workplace Torts." In *Employment Issues in Higher Education: A Legal Compendium,* edited by Jean S. Sagan and Thomas P. Rebel. Washington, D.C.: National Association of College and University Attorneys. ED 378 932. 532 pp. MF–02; PC not available EDRS.

———. 1995b. "Wrongful Termination Revisited: Just When You Thought It Was Safe to Discharge." In *Employment Issues in Higher Education: A Legal Compendium,* edited by Jean S. Sagan and Thomas P. Rebel. Washington, D.C.: National Association of College and University Attorneys. ED 378 932. 532 pp. MF–02; PC not available EDRS.

McKinney, Joseph R., and A. William Place. 1993. "Judicial Review of Arbitration Awards in the Educational Sector." *Education Law Reporter* 82: 749–59.

McLean, Timothy M. 1987. "Tort Liability of Colleges and Universities for Injuries Resulting from Student Alcohol Consumption." *Journal of College and University Law* 14(2): 399–416.

McWhirter, D.A. 1994. *Search, Seizure, and Privacy.* Phoenix: Oryx Press.

Mager, T. Richard. 1978. "A New Perspective for the First Amendment in Higher Education." In *The Legal Foundations of Student Personnel Services in Higher Education,* edited by Edward Hammond and Robert Shaffer. Washington, D.C.: American College Personnel Association.

Maguire, Daniel C. January/February 1987. "Can a University Be Catholic?" *Academe:* 12–16.

Marchese, Theodore J., and Jane F. Lawrence. 1988. *The Search Committee Handbook: A Guide to Recruiting Administrators.* Washington, D.C.: American Association for Higher Education. ED 346 760. 62 pp. MF–01; PC–03.

Martell, K., and G. Sullivan. April 1994. "Sexual Harassment: The Continuing Workplace Crisis." *Labor Law Journal* 45: 195–207.

Mawdsley, Ralph D. 1986. "Plagiarism Problems in Higher Education." *Journal of College and University Law* 12(3): 65–92.

Metzger, Walter P. 1993. "Professional and Legal Limits to Academic

Freedom." *Journal of College and University Law* 20(1): 1–14.

Milam, Steven D., and Rebecca D. Marshall. 1987. "Impact of *Regents of the University of Michigan v. Ewing* on Academic Dismissals from Graduate and Professional Schools." *Journal of College and University Law* 13(4): 335–52.

Milani, Adam A. 1996. "Disabled Students in Higher Education: Administrative and Judicial Enforcement of Disability Law." *Journal of College and University Law* 22(4): 989–1044.

Miller, Nelson P. 1990. "Subpoenas in Academia: Controlling Disclosure." *Journal of College and University Law* 17(1): 1–10.

Moll, Jon H. 1995. "Nuts and Bolts: The Employment Contract." In *Employment Issues in Higher Education: A Legal Compendium,* edited by Jean S. Sagan and Thomas P. Rebel. Washington, D.C.: National Association of College and University Attorneys. ED 378 932. 532 pp. MF–02; PC not available EDRS.

Moore, Donald R., and Eric R. Jones. 1978. "Civil Rights Legislation and Higher Education." In *The Legal Foundations of Student Personnel Services in Higher Education,* edited by Edward Hammond and Robert Shaffer. Washington, D.C.: American College Personnel Association.

Moots, Philip R. 1991. "A Fresh Look at Your Bylaws." *AGB Reports* 33(3): 24–28.

Morris, Arval A. 1996. "Separation of Church and State? Remarks on *Rosenburger v. University of Virginia." West's Education Law Quarterly* 5(1): 100–118.

Morton, Susan E. 1985. "Who Should Speak, Who Should Pay? The Complexities of Refunding Student Fees at Public Colleges and Universities." *Journal of College and University Law* 11(4): 481–99.

Mullaney, Joan Ward, and Elizabeth March Timberlake. 1994. "University Tenure and the Legal System: Procedures, Conflicts, and Resolutions." *Journal of Social Work Education* 30(2): 172–84.

Mullaney, Tim. 1993. "Gatekeeping through Termination of Unsuitable Social Work Students: Legal Issues and Guidelines." *Journal of Social Work Education* 29(2): 150–59.

National Association of Student Personnel Administrators. 1994. "Complying with the Final Regulations: The Student Right to Know and Campus Securities Act." Washington, D.C.: Author.

Neuberger, Carmen G. 1992. "Working with International Students on Our Campuses." In *Working with International Students and Scholars on American Campuses,* edited by David McIntire and Patricia Willer. Washington, D.C.: National Association of Student Personnel Administrators. ED 360 599. 193 pp. MF–01; PC–08.

Newman, Stephen A. 1995. "At Work in the Marketplace of Ideas: Academic Freedom, the First Amendment, and *Jeffries v. Harleston." Journal of College and University Law* 22(2): 281–330.

Noonan, John T. 1993. "Religious Law Schools and the First Amendment." *Journal of College and University Law* 20(1): 43–50.

Nordin, Virginia Davis. 1981. "The Contract to Educate: Toward a More Workable Theory of the Student-University Relationship." *Journal of College and University Law* 8(2): 141–81.

Oh, James J. 1992. "Internal Sexual Harassment Complaints: Investigating to Win." *Employee Relations Law Journal* 18(2): 227–44.

Olivas, Michael A. 1992. "The Political Economy of Immigration, Intellectual Property, and Racial Harassment." *Journal of Higher Education* 63(5): 570–98.

———. 1993. "Reflections on Professional Academic Freedom: Second Thoughts on the Third Essential Freedom." *Stanford Law Review* 45: 1835–58.

———. 1997. *The Law and Higher Education*. Durham, N.C.: Carolina Academic Press.

Olivas, Michael, and Augustina Reyes. 1996. "New Trouble: Teachers with Language Deficiencies." *Planning for Higher Education* 24(2): 19–26.

Olswang, Steven G. 1983. "Planning the Unthinkable: Issues in Institutional Reorganization and Faculty Reductions." *Journal of College and University Law* 9(4): 431–49.

———. 1988. "Union Security Provisions, Academic Freedom, and Tenure: The Implications of *Chicago Teachers Union v. Hudson.*" *Journal of College and University Law* 14(4): 539–60.

Olswang, Steven G., and Jane I. Fantel. 1980. "Tenure and Periodic Performance Review: Compatible Legal and Administrative Principles." *Journal of College and University Law* 7(1): 1–30.

O'Neil, Robert M. 1993. "The Lawyer and the Client in the Campus Setting: Who Is the Client, What Does the Client Expect, and How May the Attorney Respond?" *Journal of College and University Law* 19(4): 333–42.

O'Neill, Catherine A. 1997. "Single-Sex Education after *United States v. Virginia.*" *Journal of College and University Law* 23(3): 489–523.

Pacholski, Susan L. 1992. "Title VII in the University: The Difference Academic Freedom Makes." *University of Chicago Law Review* 59: 1317–36.

Page, Richard K., and Kay H. Hunnicutt. 1994. "Freedom for the Thought That We Hate: A Policy Analysis of Student Speech Regulation at America's Twenty Largest Public Universities." *Journal of College and University Law* 21(1): 1–60.

Paludi, Michele A., ed. 1996. *Sexual Harassment on College Campuses: Abusing the Ivory Power*. Albany: State Univ. of New York Press.

Papandreou, Alexander C. 1993. *"Krebs v. Rutgers:* The Potential for Disclosure of Highly Classified Personal Information Renders Questionable the Use of Social Security Numbers as Student Identification Numbers." *Journal of College and University Law*

20(1): 79–96.

Paretsky, Jonathan M. 1993. "Judicial Review of Discretionary Grants of Higher Education Tenure." *Education Law Reporter* 83: 17–26.

Parker, Craig W. 1989. "Overview of Tort Law: Concepts in Defining Liability of Colleges and Universities." In *Am I Liable? Faculty, Staff, and Institutional Liability in the College and University Setting*. Washington, D.C.: National Association of College and University Attorneys.

Parrish, Debra. 1995. "Scientific Misconduct and the Plagiarism Cases." *Journal of College and University Law* 21(3): 517–54.

Patel, Sandip H. 1995. "Graduate Students' Ownership and Attribution Rights in Intellectual Property." *Indiana Law Journal* 71: 481–512.

Pavela, Gary. 1990. "The Dismissal of Students with Mental Disorders." Washington, D.C.: National Association of College and University Attorneys.

———. 1995. "Deconstructing Academic Freedom." *Journal of College and University Law* 22(2): 359–65.

Pelesh, Mark L. 1995. "Due Process in the Accreditation Context: A Reply." *Journal of College and University Law* 22(1): 175–90.

Perry, Nancy Walker. 1993. "Sexual Harassment on Campus: Are Your Actions Actionable?" *Journal of College Student Development* 34: 406–10.

Phillips, Michael J. 1991. "The Substantive Due Process Rights of College and University Faculty." *American Business Law Journal* 28: 567–604.

Phillips, S.E. 25 March 1993. "Testing Condition Accommodations for Disabled Students." *Education Law Reporter* 80: 9–32.

Prairie, Michael W., and Lori A. Chamberlain. 1994. "Due Process in the Accreditation Context." *Journal of College and University Law* 21(1): 61–110.

Price, Sheila, and John O. Andes. 1990. "An Update on Academic Dismissal for Clinical Reasons." *Journal of Dental Education* 54(12): 747–49.

Pullum, Stephen J. 1991. "Illegal Questions in the Selection Interview: Going Beyond Contemporary Business and Professional Communication Textbooks." *Bulletin of the Association for Business Communication* 54(3): 36–43.

Radford, Mary F. 1994. "By Invitation Only: The Proof of Welcomeness in Sexual Harassment Cases." *North Carolina Law Review* 72: 499–548.

Raines, Jell B., and Lawrence F. Rossow. 1994. "The Americans with Disabilities Act: Resolving the Separate-but-Equal Problem in Colleges and Universities." *Education Law Reporter* 88(1): 308–18.

Raisfeld, Ruth D. 1994. "A Gathering Storm: Legal Issues Concerning Students with Disabilities." In *Accommodating Students with Learning and Emotional Disabilities: A Legal Compendium,* edited by Richard B. Crockett and Shelley Sanders Kehl (1996). Washington, D.C.: National Association of College and University Attorneys.

Reams, Bernard D. 1987. "Revocation of Academic Degrees by Colleges and Universities." *Journal of College and University Law* 14(2): 283–302.

Rebell, Michael A. 1991. "Teacher Performance Assessment: The Changing State of the Law." *Journal of Personnel Evaluation in Education* 5: 227–35.

Redlich, Norman. 1992. "Law School Faculty Hiring under Title VII: How a Judge Might Decide a Disparate Impact Case." *Journal of Legal Education* 41(2): 135–39.

Reidhaar, Donald L. 1985. "The Assault on the Citadel: Reflections on a Quarter Century of Change in the Relationships between the Student and the University." *Journal of College and University Law* 12(3): 343–61.

Richmond, Douglas R. 1989. "Students' Right to Counsel in University Disciplinary Proceedings." *Journal of College and University Law* 15(3): 289–312.

Rieder, Robert W., and William B. Woodward, Jr. 1993. "University Liability for Sports Injuries." *NASPA Journal* 31(1): 56–63.

Riley, Gresham. July/August 1993. "The Cost of Speech Codes." *Academe:* 26–30.

Robinson, John H., and Catherine Pieronek. 1996. "The Law of Higher Education and the Courts: 1994 in Review." *Journal of College and University Law* 22(3): 367–894.

Robinson, Robert K., Geralyn McClure Franklin, and Billie Morgan Allen. 1990. *"University of Pennsylvania v. EEOC:* The Demise of Academic Freedom Privilege in the Peer Review Process." *Labor Law Journal* 41: 364–69.

Roschwalb, Jerald. Summer 1992. "Getting Involved: CEOs and the Regulatory Process." *Educational Record* 73(3): 29–32.

Roster, Michael, and Linda Woodward. 1996. "A New Approach to Campus Legal Services." *Planning for Higher Education* 24(4): 1–4.

Roth, Stefanie H. 1994. "Sex Discrimination 101: Developing a Title IX Analysis for Sexual Harassment in Education." *Journal of Law and Education* 23(4): 459–521.

Rothstein, Laura F. 1991. "Student, Staff, and Faculty with Disabilities: Current Issues for Colleges and Universities." *Journal of College and University Law* 17(4): 471–82.

———. 1993. "College Students with Disabilities: Litigation Trends." *Review of Litigation* 13: 425–45.

———. 1994. "ADA Compliance Tasks for University Administrators." In *Accommodating Students with Learning and Emotional*

Disabilities: A Legal Compendium, edited by Richard B. Crockett and Shelley Sanders Kehl (1996). Washington, D.C.: National Association of College and University Attorneys.

———. 1995. "Current Disability Law Issues for Higher Education." In *Accommodating Students with Learning and Emotional Disabilities: A Legal Compendium,* edited by Richard B. Crockett and Shelley Sanders Kehl (1996). Washington, D.C.: National Association of College and University Attorneys.

Ruebhausen, Oscar M. 1988. "The Age Discrimination Amendments of 1986: Implications for Tenure and Early Retirement." *Journal of College and University Law* 14(4): 561–74.

Ruiz, Celia M. 1995. "Legal Standards Regarding Gender Equity and Affirmative Action." ED 381 864. 14 pp. MF–01; PC–01.

Rush, Kenneth W. 1991. "Developing a Compensation Program." In *Human Resource Management in Religiously Affiliated Institutions,* edited by Barbara Nicholson-Brown. Washington, D.C.: College and University Personnel Association.

Russo, Charles J., ed. 1996. *Yearbook of Education Law, 1996.* Dayton, Ohio: Education Law Association.

Ryan, Dan, and Maureen McCarthy, eds. 1994. *A Student Affairs Guide to the ADA and Disability Issues.* Washington, D.C.: National Association of Student Personnel Administrators.

Ryan, Nancy E. 1992. "Coping with the WARN Act." *Employee Relations Law Journal* 18(1): 169–76.

Sacken, Donal M. 1992. "Commercialization of Academic Knowledge and Judicial Deference." *Journal of College and University Law* 19(1): 1–16.

Samit, Jacob M. 1993. "Guidelines for Handling Grievances at the Formal Level." In *Managing the Industrial Labor Relations Process in Higher Education,* edited by Daniel J. Julius. Washington, D.C.: College and University Personnel Association.

Sarchet, Bruce J. 1995. "Faculty Performance Evaluations: Confidentiality, Open Records, Employment Discrimination, and Termination of Employment." In *Employment Issues in Higher Education: A Legal Compendium,* edited by Jean S. Sagan and Thomas P. Rebel. Washington, D.C.: National Association of College and University Attorneys. ED 378 932. 532 pp. MF–02; PC not available EDRS.

Saunders, Edward J. 1993. "Confronting Academic Dishonesty." *Journal of Social Work Education* 29(2): 224–31.

Saurack, Walter. 1995. "Protecting the Student: A Critique of the Procedural Protection Afforded to American and English Students in University Disciplinary Hearings." *Journal of College and University Law* 21(4): 785–824.

Schatken, Steven N. 1989. "Student Records at Institutions of Postsecondary Education: Selected Issues under the Family Educational Rights and Privacy Act of 1974." In *College and Student Records: A Legal Compendium,* edited by Joan E. Van Tol. Washington, D.C.: National Association of College and University Attorneys.

Schimmel, David. 1996. "Discrimination against Religious Viewpoints Prohibited in Public Colleges and Universities: An Analysis of *Rosenburger v. University of Virginia." West's Education Law Quarterly* 5(1): 62–68.

Schwartzman, Herbert D. 1973. "The Administration's Approach to Collective Bargaining." *Journal of College and University Law* 1(3): 351–69.

Schweitzer, Thomas A. 1992. "'Academic Challenge' Cases: Should Judicial Review Extend to Academic Evaluation of Students?" *American University Law Review* 41: 267–367.

Scott, Sally S. 1994. "Determining Reasonable Academic Adjustments for College Students with Learning Disabilities." *Journal of Learning Disabilities* 27(7): 403–12.

Serebrini, Riqua R., Suzanne E. Gordon, and Barbara A. Mann. 1994. "Student Development Theories as Related to Students with Disabilities." In *A Student Affairs Guide to the ADA and Disability Issues,* edited by Dan Ryan and Maureen McCarthy. Washington, D.C.: National Association of Student Personnel Administrators.

Shaw, Mark A. 1991. "Institutional Academic Freedom Fails to Protect Disclosures of Peer Review Evaluations: *University of Pennsylvania v. EEOC." Toledo Law Review* 22: 1089–1118.

Simon, Barbara L. 1992. "U.S. Immigration Policies, 1789–1992: Invaluable Texts for Exploring Continuity and Change in Racism and Xenophobia." *Journal of Multicultural Social Work* 2(2): 53–63.

Smith, Eugene H., and Marvin J. Baron. 1986. *Faculty Member's Guide to U.S. Immigration Law.* Washington, D.C.: National Association of Foreign Student Affairs. ED 271 063. 53 pp. MF–01; PC not available EDRS.

Smith, Evan B. 1989. "Charting Complexities of Modern Libel Law." *Educator* 44(1): 20–26.

Smith, Francis S. 1993. "Looking a Gift Horse in the Mouth." Washington, D.C.: National Association of College and University Attorneys. ED 363 181. 33 pp. MF–01; PC not available EDRS.

Smith, Michael Clay, and Richard Fossey. 1995. *Crime on Campus: Legal Issues and Campus Administration.* Phoenix: Oryx Press.

Smolla, Rodney A. 1990. "Academic Freedom, Hate Speech, and the Idea of a University." *Law and Contemporary Problems* 53(3): 195–225.

Sorenson, Gail, and Andrew S. LaManque. 1996. "The Application of *Hazelwood v. Kuhlmeier* in College Litigation." *Journal of College and University Law* 22(4): 971–88.

Stadler, James R. 1989. "Drug Testing of College and University Employees." *Journal of College and University Law* 15(3): 321–34.

Steadman, Clayton D. 1989. "Workers Compensation." In *Am I Liable? Faculty, Staff, and Institutional Liability in the College and University Setting.* Washington, D.C.: National Association of College and University Attorneys.

Stewart, David W., and Henry A. Spille. 1989. "Diploma Mills: Degrees of Fraud." In *College and Student Records: A Legal Compendium,* edited by Joan E. Van Tol. Washington, D.C.: National Association of College and University Attorneys.

Stith, Rebecca S., and William A. Kohlburn. 1992. "Early Retirement Incentive Plans after the Passage of the Older Workers Benefit Protective Act." *St. Louis University Public Law Review* 11: 263–79.

Stopp, Margaret T., and G. Harry Stopp. 1992. "The Enforcement of University Patent Policies: A Legal Perspective." *SRA Journal* 24(3): 5–11.

Stuart, Victoria. 1987. "Learning the Legalities." *Currents* 13(10): 26–29.

Sullivan, William H. 1989. "The College or University Power to withhold Diplomas." In *College and Student Records: A Legal Compendium,* edited by Joan E. Van Tol. Washington, D.C.: National Association of College and University Attorneys.

Svarney, Ronald J. 1989. "Counseling Foreign Law Students." *Journal of Counseling and Development* 68(2): 228–31.

Swan, Peter N. 1990. "Subjective Hiring and Promotion Decisions in the Wake of *Fort Worth, Atonio,* and *Price Waterhouse.*" *Journal of College and University Law* 16(4): 553–73.

———. 1992. "Early Retirement Incentives with Upper Age Limits under the Older Workers Benefits Protection Act." *Journal of College and University Law* 19(2): 53–72.

Swedlow, Kathryn R. 1994. "Suing for Tenure: Legal and Institutional Barriers." *Review of Litigation* 13: 557–95.

Swem, Lisa L. 1987. "Due Process Rights in Student Discipline Cases." *Journal of College and University Law* 14(2): 299–416.

Swenson, Elizabeth V. 1995. "Student v. Instructor: Higher Education Law in the Trenches." *Teaching of Psychology* 22(3): 169–72.

Tanner, Gerald. 1978. "Legal Aspects of Student Personnel Functions." In *The Legal Foundations of Student Personnel Services in Higher Education,* edited by Edward Hammond and Robert Shaffer. Washington, D.C.: American College Personnel Association.

Taylor, Anne. 1995. "A View from the Trenches: Current Issues in ADA Title I Compliance from the Perspective of University Counsel." In *Employment Issues in Higher Education: A Legal Compendium,* edited by Jean S. Sagan and Thomas P. Rebel. Washington, D.C.: National Association of College and University

Attorneys. ED 378 932. 532 pp. MF–02; PC not available EDRS.

Thomas, Stephen B., and Judy L. Hirschman. 1995. "Minority-Targeted Scholarships: More than a Black and White Issue." *Journal of College and University Law* 21(3): 555–90.

Thompson, Larry R. 1989. "Revocation of Degrees: Outline of Legal and Administrative Issues." In *College and Student Records: A Legal Compendium,* edited by Joan E. Van Tol. Washington, D.C.: National Association of College and University Attorneys.

Thrasher, Frederick. 1992. "The Impact of Title II and III of the Americans with Disabilities Act of 1990 on Academic and Student Services at Colleges and Proprietary Schools." In *Accommodating Students with Learning and Emotional Disabilities: A Legal Compendium,* edited by Richard B. Crockett and Shelley Sanders Kehl (1996). Washington, D.C.: National Association of College and University Attorneys.

Traynor, Michael. 1990. "Defamation Law: Shock Absorbers for the Ride into the Groves of Academe." *Journal of College and University Law* 16(3): 373–96.

Tucker, Bonnie Poitras. 1996. "Application of the Americans with Disabilities Act (ADA) and Section 504 to Colleges and Universities: An Overview and Discussion of Special Issues Relating to Students." *Journal of College and University Law* 23(1): 1–42.

Tysee, G. John, and Kimberly L. Japinga. 1993. "The Family and Medical Leave Act: Easily Conceived, Difficult Birth, Enigmatic Child." *Creighton Law Review* 27: 361–80.

U.S. Dept. of Justice. 1995. "Enforcing the ADA: A Status Report from the Department of Justice." In *Employment Issues in Higher Education: A Legal Compendium,* edited by Jean S. Sagan and Thomas P. Rebel. Washington, D.C.: National Association of College and University Attorneys. ED 378 932. 532 pp. MF–02; PC not available EDRS.

Van Alstyne, William W., ed. 1993. *Freedom and Tenure in the Academy.* Durham, N.C.: Duke Univ. Press.

Van Tol, Joan E., ed. 1989. *College and Student Records: A Legal Compendium.* Washington, D.C.: National Association of College and University Attorneys.

Volokh, Eugene. 1992. "Freedom of Speech and Workplace Harassment." *UCLA Law Review* 39: 1791–1872.

Wagner, Eileen N. 1991. "Beware the Custom-Made Anthology: Academic Photocopying and *Basic Books v. Kinko's Graphics.*" *West's Education Law Reporter* 68(1): 1–20.

Wagner, Thomas E. 1982. "Managing Legal Issues at the Departmental Level." *ADE Bulletin* 71: 25–26.

Walsh, William. 1994. "*Smith v. Regents of the University of California:* The Marketplace Is Closed." *Journal of College and University Law* 21(2): 405–19.

Walton, Spring J. 1992. "In Loco Parentis for the 1990s: New Liabilities." *Ohio Northern University Law Review* 19: 247–70.

Walworth, Carla R., and Margaret J. Strange. 1992–93. "Serving Two Masters: The Interaction between Family and Medical Leave Acts and the ADA." *Employee Relations Law Journal* 18(3): 461–78.

Ware, David, Patricia Somers, and Scott Speake. Summer 1993. "Immigration Law and Higher Education: Employment of International Employees." *Journal of College and University Law* 20(1).

Ware, Leland. 1996. "Tales from the Crypt: Does Strict Scrutiny Sound the Death Knell for Affirmative Action in Higher Education?" *Journal of College and University Law* 23(1): 43–90.

Weeks, Kent M. 1990. "The Peer Review Process." *Journal of Higher Education* 61(2): 198–219.

Wells, Anne, and John L. Strope, Jr. 1996. "The *Podberesky* Case and Race-Related Financial Aid." *Journal of Student Financial Aid* 26(1): 33–43.

Wenkart, Ronald D. 1993. "The Americans with Disabilities Act and Its Impact on Public Education." *Education Law Reporter* 82: 291–302.

White, Lawrence. 1989. "Complying with the 'Drug-Free Workplace' Laws on College and University Campuses." Washington, D.C.: National Association of College and University Attorneys. ED 410 850. 31 pp. MF–01; PC not available EDRS.

White, Wendy S. 1993. "Current Legal Issues Affecting Admissions Programs, Including the Bona Fides of Physical and Mental Capacity Requirements; the 'Learning Disabled' Applicant; Are Certain Resources Mandated by the 'Reasonable Accommodation' Requirement?" In *Accommodating Students with Learning and Emotional Disabilities: A Legal Compendium,* edited by Richard B. Crockett and Shelley Sanders Kehl (1996). Washington, D.C.: National Association of College and University Attorneys.

Wiltbank, J. Kelley, ed. 1990. "The Practical Aspects of Technology Transfer: A Legal Compendium." Washington, D.C.: National Association of College and University Attorneys.

Yeung, Timothy G. 1995. "Discovery of Confidential Peer Review Materials in Title VII Actions for Unlawful Denial of Tenure: A Case against Redaction." *U.C.–Davis Law Review* 29: 167–95.

Young, D. Parker. 1978. "Student Personnel Staff Liability." In *The Legal Foundations of Student Personnel Services in Higher Education,* edited by Edward Hammond and Robert Shaffer. Washington, D.C.: American College Personnel Association.

Zirkel, Perry A. 1985. "Personality as a Fourth Criterion for Tenure." *Phi Kappa Phi Journal* 65(1): 34–46.

Zirkel, Perry A., and Paul S. Hugel. 1989. "Academic Misguidance in Colleges and Universities." *Education Law Reporter* 56(3): 709–30.

INDEX

A

AAUP
> 1915 Declaration of Principles, 61
> 1940 Statement of Principles, 27–28, 60–61

abstention doctrine, 33

academic administrators
> encourage to be active participants in resolving legal issues, 1
> following own rules likely upheld by the courts, 89
> sources of information available on higher education law, 2–3
> what need to know regarding law, 5

academic freedom, 60–64
> Justice Frankfurter portrayal of, 61–62
> less developed for students than for institutions or faculty, 60
> principles reflecting First Amendment ideals, 7
> social rationale for, 60

academic self-government (=*freiheit der wessenschaft*), 60

basis of academic freedom, 60

accreditation, 121–22

accrediting agencies not subject to constitutional provisions, 121

ADA. *See* Americans with Disabilities Act.

Adarand Constructors, Inc. v. Pena (1995), 39

ADEA. *See* Age Discrimination in Employment Act.

adequate cause for dismissal determination requirements, 76–77

admissions and access, 93
> equal protection principle, permitted departures from, 94

affirmative action, 39–42
> definition of good faith effort regarding, 54
> four requirements of voluntary, 41
> not required by Americans with Disabilities Act, 37
> permissible provided two conditions are met, 95

age discrimination
> preventive measures, 38–39

Age Discrimination in Employment Act (ADEA), 7, 37–39, 65, 82
> under 1986 amendment no longer can compel retirement, 84

allegation of scientific misconduct, first institutional step, 117

amendment freedoms most significant for administration, 8

American College Personnel Association (ACPA), 3

Americans with Disabilities Act (ADA), 7, 34–37, 97
> disabilities under, 35, 98
> effect of, 97
> protects against discrimination on basis of addiction, 57
> qualifications for protection under, 34

---

animal rights rules, 118

answer as type of document in pretrial procedure, 17

antidiscrimination laws apply regardless of funding source, 13

antitrust laws held to apply to higher education, 97

apparent authority, 23

appropriate measures to ensure due process in accreditation, 122

arrest records questions, 54

attorney

    -client relationship, 14–17

    fees in judgment, 22

    "work product," 20

authority

    types, 23

    vested in governing board, 22

auxiliary service when exempt from local taxation, 119–20

B

"balance test," 117

bargaining unit, 29

Basic Books v. Kinko's Graphics Corp. (1991), 111–13

Bill of Rights does not apply to private institutions, 13

Board of Regents v. Roth (1972), 75–76

Bob Jones University v. United States (1983), 14, 51

Brigham Young University, 49

Buckley Amendment. *See* Family Education Rights and Privacy
    Act of 1974 (FERPA).

C

Calvin College, 49

campus common law, 9

campus housing used by presidents held to be tax exempt, 120

Catholic University of America, 49

charitable immunity doctrine, 10

church-related institutions

    allowed to discriminate somewhat in hiring, 50–51

Citadel, 96

City of Richmond v. J.A. Crowson Co. (1989), 39

Civil Rights Act of 1964, 94

Civil Rights Act of 1990, 38

civil rights legislation enforcement as area of state involvement, 10

claim preclusion, 21

Clark v. Community for Creative Non-Violence (1984), 103

collective bargaining, 29–30

College and University Personnel Association (CUPA), 3
college presidents' tax-exempt campus housing, 120
common law as a source of law, 9
community college officials
        often not considered alter egos of the state, 24
"community of interest," 29
compelling justification standard, 40
compensatory damages, 21
conduct and misconduct on the job, 60–74
confidentiality dilemma, 118
confidentiality of attorney-client relationship, 15
Connick v. Myers (1983), 63
constitutional
        issues that can originate among units in higher education, 6–7
        provisions only protect against the state, 6
contract, 5–6
        law as limit of the protection of academic freedom, 61
        ways of changing or voiding, 28
        wrongful dismissal actions, 80–81
contract theory
        affords students considerable protection, 87
        successful challenge of administration by students using, 90
contractual
        expectations of staff and non tenured faculty, creation of
            enforceable, 80
        issues deans and chairs commonly confront, 5
        relationships for employment, 27–29
copyright
        obtaining permission, 113
Copyright Act of 1976, 111
Copyright Clearance Center, 113
counsel
        institutional expectations of, 15
        loyalty to the institution and not to individuals, 16
courts
        rationale for not hearing a case, 18–19
        usually upheld any reason for denying tenure, 44
CUPA. *See* College and University Personnel Association.

D
deans' and chairs' duties, emphasis on topics within the scope of, 2
decree document, 21
defamation, 73–75

defense made on basis of privilege, 73–74
four standards in liability for defamation, 73
misconduct that would be classified as a tort, 6
deference to academic and behavioral decisions, 9–12
delegated powers theory, 13
depositions, 20
designated school official (DSO)
monitor status of foreign students, 101
disability, 97–100
disadvantages often accompanying openness and disclosure at
public institutions, 115
disciplinary
codes, criteria for regular review of, 93
procedures, need for progressive, 38
discovery, 19–20
discrimination, 94–97
against smokers, 52
based on physical appearance not prohibited, 53
lawsuits regarding tenure, 44
on basis of addiction, 57
dismissal and retirement of faculty and staff, 74–84
dismissal
more likely approved by judicial review if product of
system of evaluation linked with faculty development,
65–66
of staff and nontenured faculty, 79–84
of tenured faculty for cause and financial exigency, 75–79
disparate impact, 32–33
theory, 84
treatment, 32
treatment theory, 84
under the Age Discrimination in Employment Act, 65
Dixon v. Alabama State Board of Education (1961), 86
document requests, 20
drug-free workplace, effect of federal legislation requiring, 115
drug testing as a Fourth Amendment issue, 56
due process
as constitutional-type issue, 7
as greatest area of potential uncertainty and difficulty in
disciplinary actions, 91
property interest as basis of, 91
requirements must be met when considering discipline or
dismissal, 72

requirements often of limited use in admissions challenges, 94

rights of students, 91

E

Educational Amendments of 1972, 94

educational status and work experience, questions on, 53

EEOC. *See* Equal Employment Opportunity Commission.

Eleventh Amendment

 immunity for infringement lawsuits eliminated, 113–114

 protection, 24–25

employee

 benefits issues often contractual in nature, 6

 handbook, incorporation into contract of, 27

 misconduct, 65–73

employment

 academics have a limited right to outside, 62

 contract, personnel issues often rely on interpretations of, 6

 contract, should refer to, 28

 discrimination case proof, 31

 evaluation as slander, 74

 evaluation use, 38

 grievance and arbitration procedures, 6

 interviews, 51–56

 references, standards for, 74–75

employment-at-will doctrine, 79–81

employment relationship. *See* conduct and misconduct on the job.

English proficiency laws, 119

Equal Employment Opportunity Commission (EEOC), 8, 31

 can subpoena files in investigating discrimination in a

  tenure case, 46

 enforces Americans with Disabilities Act, 34

Equal Pay Act, 32

Equal Protection Clause of the Fourteenth Amendment, 31, 32, 94

 public institutions subject to, 93

equal protection principle, permitted departures from , 94

Establishment Clause test, 14

estoppel, 24

ethical dilemmas for campus counsel, 16–17

express authority, 23

expression proffered by public institutions

 three-part test for upholding regulations relating to, 103–4

external regulations and institutional self-regulation as factors increasing litigation, 12

F

facilities modification to ensure reasonable access, 98–99
faculty
    activities and interests subject to three-stage analysis, 63
    bargaining units, 29
fair use, what constitutes, 112–13
Family and Medical Leave Act of 1993, 115
    eligibility requirements, 115–16
Family Education Rights and Privacy Act of 1974 (FERPA), 101, 102
    controls access to student records, 101
federal statutes
    aimed at eliminating discrimination can apply to both
        public and private institutions, 7
    exceptions to the at-will doctrine, 82
Fifth Amendment rights, 8
financial
    aid, 101
    exigency as cause for dismissal of tenured faculty, 79
First Amendment
    applies only to public restrictions on protected activity, 103
    legal definition of academic freedom centered in, 61
    must recognize right to organize, 104
    rights, 8
fiscal exigency determination, 78–79
four fair use factors difficult to apply because they are interdependent, 113
Fourteenth Amendment
    guarantees as basis for allegations of discrimination, 6
    legal definition of academic freedom centered in, 61
    rights, 8
Fourth Amendment
    enters into higher education in two principal ways, 55–56
    rights, 8
"fraud in the inducement" causes contract to be considered as
    never existing, 28
Free Exercise Clause, 14
freedom to protest not the freedom to disrupt, 104
freiheit der wessenschaft. See academic self-government.
Full Faith and Credit Clause of the U.S. Constitution, 21

G

*Gay Rights Coalition of Georgetown University Law Center v.
Georgetown University* (1987), 106

gender

-based wage discrimination, 66

classifications, legality of plan for, 41–42

general due process principles, 92

Goldfarb v. Virginia State Bar (1975), 96

"good cause"

need for in dismissing employees for alleged misconduct, 72

governing boards, responsibilities of, 22

government contacts theory, 13

governmental immunity

doctrine of, 10

only protects institutions, 24

grievance procedures, 73

Griswold v. Connecticut (1965), 57

Gustavus Adolphus College, 49

H

H-1B nonimmigrant visa, 59

Harvard University, 49

Harris v. Forklift Systems (1986), 70

"hate speech," lack of protection, 103–4

Healy v. James (1972), 104

Hendrickson, Robert

Yearbook of Education Law, 2

higher education law, sources of information on, 2–3

hiring and promotion decisions

equal protection and due process, 30–51

practical concerns, 51–60

Hopwood v. State of Texas (1996), 95

horizontal monopoly, 97

hostile work environment as sexual harassment, 66

human subjects in research rules, 118

I

immigration, 57–60

and international students, 100–1

Immigration Act of 1990, 58

Immigrations and Naturalization Act of 1952, 58

Immigration Marriage Fraud Act, 58

Immigration Reform and Control Act of 1986 (IRCA), 58

immorality, determination of, 78

implied authority, 23

incompetence, determination of, 77

individual board members shielded from personal liability, 22–23

individual or institutional liability, 22–25

individual privacy rights, 56–57

inherent authority, 23

in-house counsel, 14

injunctive relief, 22

in loco parentis

    called into question in the 1960s, 86

In re Atlantic Coast Conference (1993), 119

INS form I-20AB, 100

institutional

    accreditation, 121

    custom determines where misconduct is punished, 90

    formal procedures in a sexual harassment–based lawsuit, 67–68

    liability, 108–9

    needs as support for negative tenure decisions, 44

    obligation in a potential sexual harassment–based lawsuit, 67

    rules as guidelines to survive legal challenges, 91

institutions

    legitimately may refuse to hire any person with a disability, 36

    liable in a sexual harassment–based lawsuit, 67

    need to be especially watchful when accepting outside gifts likely to offend government or charter restrictions, 120

insubordination

    cases, 77

    determination of, 78

internal staff meetings

    usually not covered under open meetings legislation, 114

interrogatories, 20

J

job description, importance of, 35

Johnson v. Transportation Agency, Santa Clara County (1987), 40

Journal of College and University Law, 2–3

judicial deference tradition, 10

jurisdiction questions, 18

Justice Frankfurter on academic freedom, 61–62

L

landlord-tenant relationship

    institutional duty to students in area of liability likened to, 108

Law and Higher Education, 2
Law of Higher Education, 2
law, sources of, 8
lawsuits, avoiding, 49
learning disabilities, 98
learning freedom (*lernfreiheit*), 60
        basic of academic freedom, 60
legal
        best way to address concerns, 1
        definition of academic freedom, 60–61
        difficulties in a search, ways to avoid, 56
legal issues
        rationale for exploration of, 1
        types of, 5–8
lehrfreiheit. See teaching freedom.
lernfreiheit. See learning freedom.
libel, 73
libel and obscenity, student publications subject to laws on, 107
litigation, factors that increased, 11–12
long-arm statutes, 18

M
malice, need to prove, 74
mandatory injunction, 22
mandatory retirement, 84
mandatory student activity fees, when can disallow, 106
manifest mismanagement, 22
*Marjorie Webster Junior College v. Middle States Assn. of Colleges
    and Secondary Schools* (1969), 122
Marlboro Corp. v. Assn. of Independent Colleges and Schools
    (1977), 122
means of collecting information during discovery, 20
Meritor Savings Bank v. Vinson (1986), 70
misconduct and discipline, 89–93
Mississippi University for Women v. Hogan (1982), 41–42
money damages as remedy, 21
mootness as barrier to access, 19
moral turpitude, 77
motion *in limine,* 21

N
National Association of College and University Attorneys (NACUA), 3
National Association of Student Personnel Administrators (NASPA), 3

National Collegiate Athletic Association (NCAA)
    as a vertical monopoly, 97
National Labor Relations Act, 82
    rules on collective bargaining, 29
National Labor Relations Board (NLRB), 8
        jurisdiction denied at church-related institutions, 30
        will recognize community of interest, 29
national origin, employers may not discriminate on basis of, 53
National Science Foundation and scientific misconduct, 118
National Treasury Employees Union v. Von Raabe (1989), 56–57
negligence, need to prove, 74
negligent hiring, emerging law, 54
        v. Yeshiva University (1980), 29–30
NLRB
nonimmigrant status, 58–59
nonmanagement, 23
nontenured employees have no legitimate expectations of tenure, 47

O
Oberlin College, 49
Occupational Safety and Health Administration inspections, 115
Office of Research Integrity, 118
official immunity doctrine, 24
open meetings laws, 114
openness and disclosure, 114–15
outside grants and gifts, problems with, 120–21

P
Papish v. Board of Curators of the University of Missouri (1973), 107
*Parsons College v. North Central Assn. of Colleges and Secondary
    Schools* (1967), 122
patent, 114
performance
        evaluations, post-tenure review, and comparable worth,
            63–65
        reviews, practices used to minimize legal exposure for, 64–65
        standards, courts increasingly holding all employees to, 35-36
Perry v. Sindermann (1972), 75–76
personal jurisdiction, 18
personnel issues
        and interpretations of employment contracts, 6
        at religious institutions, 49–51
physically blocking a person's access as sexual harassment, 69

Pickering v. Board of Education (1968), 63
Podberesky v. Kirwan (1991), 96
polygraph examinations, limitations, 54
post-tenure review criteria, 65
precautions against defamation, 74
precedent, 9
pretrial and trial procedures, 17–22
private action to become state action, 13
private single-sex colleges
  exempt from sex discrimination legislation, 96
privileged information between counsel and client, 5
professional definition of academic freedom, 61
prohibitory injunction, 22
program accreditation, 121
property interest as basis of due process requirements, 91
psychological disabilities, 98
public displays of nude or seminude pinups as sexual harassment,
 69
public figure and defamation, 74
public function theory, 13
public-private distinction, 12–14
punitive damages, 21

Q
qualified privilege in defamation, 72–73
quid pro quo sexual harassment, 66, 69

R
race-based
  affirmative action programs exception to general principle
   of equal protection, 94
  hiring and promotion program, 40–41
  scholarship, challenge to, 96
racial equality in education
  interest in overrides free exercise of religious rights, 51
reappointment, tenure, and promotion, 42–49
"reasonable woman" as standard in sexual harassment cases, 67
recession as a means of changing or voiding a contract, 28
recovery in defamation cases, 73
Refugee Act of 1989, 58
refusing court order to protect confidentiality, 118
Regents of the University of California v. Bakke (1978), 40, 95
Regents of the University of Michigan v. Ewing (1985), 91

Rehabilitation Act of 1973, Section 504, 97
regulations relating to expression and assembly, 103–4
religion, main types of institutions having connections with, 49–50
religious institutions
    can refuse employees based on personal conduct, 51
    expressly excluded from AAUP Statement, 61
    under protection of First Amendment, 14
religious preference questions, 53–54
remedy types, 21–22
repeated requests for dates as sexual harassment, 70
res judicata, 21
research and teaching, 116–19
research data, ownership and access, 116, 117
research documents at public institutions
    state legislation protecting, 117
reverse discrimination, 39
right of assembly as constitutional-type issue, 7
right of expression as constitutional-type issue, 7
"role models" for students not likely to support a gender-based
    affirmative action program in the academic setting, 41
roles of university counsel, 15
Rosenburger v. Rector and Visitors of the University of Virginia
    (1994), 105–6
rule of confidentiality, exception to, 15
rules and regulations, requirements to survive legal challenge, 91

S
"safe harbor" for affirmative action employment decisions virtually
    impossible, 39
scientific misconduct, 118
Section 504 expands protection, 34
Section 1981 claims, 33–34
self-dealing, 23
sex-based harassment
    circumstances of, 66
    defined under Title VII, 66
    formal procedures addressing, 68
    inappropriate attention regarding students, 70
    indirect forms of, 71
    internal sanctions or remedies resulting from, 71–72
    must be severe and pervasive, 70
    need for institutions to establish concrete policies on, 67
    prevention of, 71

relevant issues regarding an investigation of, 68

repeated requests for dates as, 70

several forms of, 69–70

sexual orientation not recognized in federal law as a class protected from discrimination, 53

Shamloo v. Mississippi State Board of Trustees (1980), 103

single-sex public institutions, 96

Skinner v. Railway Labor Executives Association (1989), 57

slander, 73

sources of

individual rights available to students and employees at private institutions, 13–14

of information on higher education law, 2–3

Southeastern Community College v. Davis (1979), 35

standard for dismissing employees for alleged misconduct, 72, 77

"standing" concept, 19

state action in private education, determination of, 13

state in education, factors leading to greater involvement, 11–12

statute of limitation as barrier to access, 19

strict scrutiny standard in affirmative action cases, 40

student organizations, 104–6

student publications, 107

student records, 101–3

conditions under which can provide access, 102

restriction of access to, 102–3

student religious groups, limitations on rights of, 105

student rights

not only contractual relative to institutions but under constitutions and statues, 88

to organize, conditions under which institutions may restrict, 104–5

students as consumers, 85

"sunshine laws." *See* open meetings laws.

Sweezy v. New Hampshire (1957), 9, 61–62

T

Taft-Hartley Act, 30

tax issues involved in employing foreign nationals, 60

taxation and fundraising, 119–21

teaching freedom (*lehrfreiheit*), 60

basis of academic freedom, 60

U.S. Supreme Court has never spoken categorically on, 62

tenure

academic qualifications for, 43
conditions under which discrimination as reason for rejecting
will not be successful, 45–46
courts exceedingly reluctant to upset administrative
evaluations for, 44–45
factors that shape decisions on, 42–43
nontenured employees have no legitimate expectation of, 47
only two circumstances for dismissing tenured faculty,
74–75
situations that can precipitate lawsuits regarding, 48–49
up-or-out proposition, 43
terminating an individual employee, 82–83
test for affirmative action
four factors, 40–41
three principal models for provision of legal services in higher
education, 14
three-stage analysis to determine of faculty activities and interests
protection, 63
Title VII of the 1964 Civil Rights Act, 82
claims, 32–33
Title IX claims, 33
tolling as mechanism to delay statute of limitation's running, 19
tort of battery, hugging as, 71
torts
involve duties that are not contractual in nature, 6
theories that challenge the traditional at-will rule, 81–82
trademark, 114
traditional legislative and judicial deference to academic decision
making, 5
trial by jury, right to, 38
two-part process for determining whether termination proceedings
should be brought against a tenured faculty member, 77–78

U

undocumented aliens, 59
United Mine Workers v. Gibbs (1966), 18
United States constitution not applicable to private institutions, 13
University of California Board of Regents' edict to end affirmative
action applies only in University of California system, 95
University of Pennsylvania v. EEOC (1990), 46–47
University of Texas law school overturning affirmative action
program, 95
unpaid leave requirement, 115–116

updates on legal issues of note to academic administrators, 3
urinalysis as a significant intrusion into a fundamentally private
    domain, 56

V

vagueness and overbreadth, 7
verbal harassment as sexual harassment, 69
vicarious liability, 54
videotape showing may also be copyright issue, 113
Virginia Military Institute, 96
voluntary efforts to address a manifest racial imbalance, 41

W

Wagner Act, 30
Ward v. Rock Against Racism (1989), 103
Weber v. Kaiser Aluminum Co. (1979), 41
Widmar v. Vincent (1981), 105
Worldwide Volkswagen Corp. v. Woodson (1980), 18
wrongful dismissal actions, precautions to minimize, 80
Wygant v. Jackson Board of Education (1986), 39

Y

Yearbook of Education Law, 2

ASHE-ERIC HIGHER EDUCATION REPORTS

Since 1983, the Association for the Study of Higher Education (ASHE) and the Educational Resources Information Center (ERIC) Clearinghouse on Higher Education, a sponsored project of the Graduate School of Education and Human Development at The George Washington University, have cosponsored the ASHE-ERIC Higher Education Report series. This volume is the twenty-sixth overall and the ninth to be published by the Graduate School of Education and Human Development at The George Washington University.

Each monograph is the definitive analysis of a tough higher education problem, based on thorough research of pertinent literature and institutional experiences. Topics are identified by a national survey. Noted practitioners and scholars are then commissioned to write the reports, with experts providing critical reviews of each manuscript before publication.

Eight monographs (10 before 1985) in the ASHE-ERIC Higher Education Report series are published each year and are available on individual and subscription bases. To order, use the order form on the last page of this book.

Qualified persons interested in writing a monograph for the ASHE-ERIC Higher Education Report series are invited to submit a proposal to the National Advisory Board. As the preeminent literature review and issue analysis series in higher education, the Higher Education Reports are guaranteed wide dissemination and national exposure for accepted candidates. Execution of a monograph requires at least a minimal familiarity with the ERIC database, including *Resources in Education* and the current *Index to Journals in Education*. The objective of these reports is to bridge conventional wisdom with practical research. Prospective authors are strongly encouraged to call at (800) 773-3742 ext. 14.

For further information, write to
    ASHE-ERIC Higher Education Report Series
    The George Washington University
    One Dupont Circle, Suite 630
    Washington, DC 20036-1183
Or phone (202) 296-2597
Toll free: (800) 773-ERIC

Write or call for a complete catalog.

Visit our Web site at **www.eriche.org**

ADVISORY BOARD

James Earl Davis
University of Delaware at Newark

Kenneth A. Feldman
State University of New York–Stony Brook

Kassie Freeman
Peabody College, Vanderbilt University

Susan Frost
Emory University

Kenneth P. Gonzalez
Arizona State University

Esther E. Gotlieb
West Virginia University

Philo Hutcheson
Georgia State University

Lori White
Stanford University

CONSULTING EDITORS

Thomas A. Angelo
University of Miami

Sandra Beyer
University of Texas at El Paso

Robert Boice
State University of New York–Stony Brook

Ivy E. Broder
The American University

Dennis Brown
Michigan State University

Shirley M. Clark
Oregon State System of Higher Education

Robert A. Cornesky
Cornesky and Associates, Inc.

K. Patricia Cross
Scholar in Residence

Rhonda Martin Epper
State Higher Education Executive Officers

Cheryl Falk
Yakima Valley Community College

Anne H. Frank
American Association of University Professors

Mildred Garcia
Arizona State University–West

Michelle D. Gilliard
Consortium for the Advancement of Private Higher
  Education–The Council of Independent Colleges

Dean L. Hubbard
Northwest Missouri State University

Lisa R. Lattuca
The Spencer Foundation, Chicago, Illinois

J. Roderick Lauver
Planned Systems International, Inc.–Maryland

Daniel T. Layzell
MGT of America, Inc., Madison, Wisconsin

Barbara Lee
Rutgers University

Ivan B. Liss
Radford University

Clara M. Lovett
Northern Arizona University

Meredith Ludwig
American Association of State Colleges and Universities

Laurence R. Marcus
Rowan College

William McKeachie
University of Michigan

Robert Menges
Northwestern University

Diane E. Morrison
Centre for Curriculum, Transfer, and Technology

John A. Muffo
Virginia Polytechnic Institute and State University

Patricia H. Murrell
University of Memphis

L. Jackson Newell
University of Utah

Steven G. Olswang
University of Washington

R. Eugene Rice
American Association for Higher Education

Sherry Sayles-Folks
Eastern Michigan University

John Schub
Wichita State University

Jack H. Schuster
Claremont Graduate School–Center for Educational Studies

Patricia Somers
University of Arkansas at Little Rock

Leonard Springer
University of Wisconsin–Madison

Marilla D. Svinicki
University of Texas–Austin

David Sweet
OERI, U.S. Department of Education

Jon E. Travis
Texas A&M University

Dan W. Wheeler
University of Nebraska–Lincoln

Donald H. Wulff
University of Washington

Manta Yorke
Liverpool John Moores University

REVIEW PANEL

Richard Alfred
University of Michigan

Robert J. Barak
Iowa State Board of Regents

Alan Bayer
Virginia Polytechnic Institute and State University

John P. Bean
Indiana University–Bloomington

John M. Braxton
Peabody College, Vanderbilt University

Ellen M. Brier
Tennessee State University

Dennis Brown
University of Kansas

Patricia Carter
University of Michigan

John A. Centra
Syracuse University

Paul B. Chewning
Council for the Advancement and Support of Education

Arthur W. Chickering
Vermont College

Darrel A. Clowes
Virginia Polytechnic Institute and State University

Deborah M. DiCroce
Piedmont Virginia Community College

Dorothy E. Finnegan
The College of William & Mary

Kenneth C. Green
Claremont Graduate University

James C. Hearn
University of Georgia

Edward R. Hines
Illinois State University

Deborah Hunter
University of Vermont

Linda K. Johnsrud
University of Hawaii at Manoa

Bruce Anthony Jones
University of Missouri–Columbia

Elizabeth A. Jones
West Virginia University

Marsha V. Krotseng
State College and University Systems of West Virginia

George D. Kuh
Indiana University–Bloomington

J. Roderick Lauver
Planned Systems International, Inc.–Maryland

Daniel T. Layzell
MGT of America, Inc., Madison, Wisconsin

Patrick G. Love
Kent State University

Meredith Jane Ludwig
American Association of State Colleges and Universities

Mantha V. Mehallis
Florida Atlantic University

Toby Milton
Essex Community College

John A. Muffo
Virginia Polytechnic Institute and State University

L. Jackson Newell
Deep Springs College

Mark Oromaner
Hudson Community College

James C. Palmer
Illinois State University

Robert A. Rhoads
Michigan State University

G. Jeremiah Ryan
Quincy College

Mary Ann Danowitz Sagaria
The Ohio State University

Kathryn Nemeth Tuttle
University of Kansas

Volume 26 ASHE-ERIC Higher Education Reports

1. Faculty Workload Studies: Perspectives, Needs, and Future Directions
   Katrina A. Meyer

2. Assessing Faculty Publication Productivity: Issues of Equity
   Elizabeth G. Creamer

3. Proclaiming and Sustaining Excellence: Assessment as a Faculty Role
   Karen Maitland Schilling and Karl L. Schilling

4. Creating Learning Centered Classrooms: What Does Learning Theory Have to Say?
   Frances K. Stage, Patricia A. Muller, Jillian Kinzie, and Ada Simmons

Volume 25 ASHE-ERIC Higher Education Reports

1. A Culture for Academic Excellence: Implementing the Quality Principles in Higher Education
   Jann E. Freed, Marie R. Klugman, and Jonathan D. Fife

2. From Discipline to Development: Rethinking Student Conduct in Higher Education
   Michael Dannells

3. Academic Controversy: Enriching College Instruction through Intellectual Conflict
   David W. Johnson, Roger T. Johnson, and Karl A. Smith

4. Higher Education Leadership: Analyzing the Gender Gap
   Luba Chliwniak

5. The Virtual Campus: Technology and Reform in Higher Education
   Gerald C. Van Dusen

6. Early Intervention Programs: Opening the Door to Higher Education
   Robert H. Fenske, Christine A. Geranios, Jonathan E. Keller, and David E. Moore

7. The Vitality of Senior Faculty Members: Snow on the Roof—Fire in the Furnace
   Carole J. Bland and William H. Bergquist

8. A National Review of Scholastic Achievement in General Education: How Are We Doing and Why Should We Care?
   Steven J. Osterlind

Volume 24 ASHE-ERIC Higher Education Reports

1. Tenure, Promotion, and Reappointment: Legal and Administrative Implications
   Benjamin Baez and John A. Centra

2. Taking Teaching Seriously: Meeting the Challenge of Instructional Improvement
   Michael B. Paulsen and Kenneth A. Feldman

3. Empowering the Faculty: Mentoring Redirected and Renewed
   Gaye Luna and Deborah L. Cullen

4. Enhancing Student Learning: Intellectual, Social, and Emotional Integration
   Anne Goodsell Love and Patrick G. Love

5. Benchmarking in Higher Education: Adapting Best Practices to Improve Quality
   Jeffrey W. Alstete

6. Models for Improving College Teaching: A Faculty Resource
   Jon E. Travis

7. Experiential Learning in Higher Education: Linking Classroom and Community
   Jeffrey A. Cantor

8. Successful Faculty Development and Evaluation: The Complete Teaching Portfolio
   John P. Murray

Volume 23 ASHE-ERIC Higher Education Reports

1. The Advisory Committee Advantage: Creating an Effective Strategy for Programmatic Improvement
   Lee Teitel

2. Collaborative Peer Review: The Role of Faculty in Improving College Teaching
   Larry Keig and Michael D. Waggoner

3. Prices, Productivity, and Investment: Assessing Financial Strategies in Higher Education
   Edward P. St. John

4. The Development Officer in Higher Education: Toward an Understanding of the Role
   Michael J. Worth and James W. Asp II

5. Measuring Up: The Promises and Pitfalls of Performance Indicators in Higher Education
   Gerald Gaither, Brian P. Nedwek, and John E. Neal

6. A New Alliance: Continuous Quality and Classroom Effectiveness
   Mimi Wolverton

7. Redesigning Higher Education: Producing Dramatic Gains in Student Learning
   Lion F. Gardiner

8. Student Learning outside the Classroom: Transcending Artificial Boundaries
   George D. Kuh, Katie Branch Douglas, Jon P. Lund, and Jackie Ramin-Gyurnek

Volume 22 ASHE-ERIC Higher Education Reports

1. The Department Chair: New Roles, Responsibilities, and Challenges
   Alan T. Seagren, John W. Creswell, and Daniel W. Wheeler

2. Sexual Harassment in Higher Education: From Conflict to Community
   Robert O. Riggs, Patricia H. Murrell, and JoAnne C. Cutting

3. Chicanos in Higher Education: Issues and Dilemmas for the 21st Century
   Adalberto Aguirre, Jr., and Ruben O. Martinez

4. Academic Freedom in American Higher Education: Rights, Responsibilities, and Limitations
   Robert K. Poch

5. Making Sense of the Dollars: The Costs and Uses of Faculty Compensation
   Kathryn M. Moore and Marilyn J. Amey

6. Enhancing Promotion, Tenure, and Beyond: Faculty Socialization as a Cultural Process
   William G. Tierney and Robert A. Rhoads

7. New Perspectives for Student Affairs Professionals: Evolving Realities, Responsibilities, and Roles
   Peter H. Garland and Thomas W. Grace

8. Turning Teaching into Learning: The Role of Student Responsibility in the Collegiate Experience
   Todd M. Davis and Patricia Hillman Murrell

Quantity

_____ Please begin my subscription to the current year's
ASHE-ERIC Higher Education Reports at $144.00, 25%
off the cover price, starting with Report 1.   _____

_____ Please send a complete set of Volume 27 (Year 2000)
ASHE-ERIC Higher Education Reports at $144.00, over
25% off the cover price.   _____

Individual reports are available for $24.00 and include the cost of shipping and handling.

SECURE ON-LINE ORDERING
**is now available on our
web site.
www.eriche.org/reports**

SHIPPING POLICY:

- Books are sent UPS Ground or equivalent. For faster delivery, call for charges. Alaska, Hawaii, U.S. Territories, and Foreign Countries, please call for shipping information. Order will be shipped within 24 hours after receipt of request. Orders of 10 or more books, call for shipping information. All prices shown are subject to change.
- Returns: No cash refunds—credit will be applied to future orders.

PLEASE SEND ME THE FOLLOWING REPORTS:

Quantity	Volume/No.	Title	Amount

Please check one of the following:

☐ Check enclosed, payable to GW-ERIC.   **Subtotal:** _____

☐ Purchase order attached.   **Less Discount:** _____

☐ Charge my credit card indicated below: **Total Due:** _____
  ☐ Visa   ☐ MasterCard

Expiration Date_____

Name_____

Title _____ E-mail _____

Institution _____

Address_____

City _____ State _____ Zip_____

Phone _____ Fax _____Telex_____

Signature _____ Date_____

SEND ALL ORDERS TO:
ASHE-ERIC Higher Education Reports Series
One Dupont Cir., Ste. 630, Washington, DC 20036-1183
Phone: (202) 296-2597 ext. 13 Toll-free: (800) 773-ERIC ext. 13
FAX: (202) 452-1844
EMAIL: order@eric-he.edu
Secure on-line ordering at URL: www.eriche.org/reports

**On-line ordering
is now available:
visit our web site at
www.eriche.org.**